Perennials...What you need to know!

Perennials...
What you need to know!

Tips and Advice to Grow
Tried and True Perennials

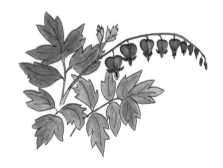

Althea R. Griffin
Gardener

Illustrated by Kate Ruland

Published by Plant It Publishing, Atlanta, Georgia

ISBN 978-0-9832347-0-8

NOTE: Reference works about perennials do not always agree with regard to botanical nomenclature, and the nomenclature is constantly evolving. Please realize the names of plants, care instructions and results in this book may differ from other gardeners' experiences, including information from other reference books, growers, plant societies and authors.

llustrations by Kate Ruland, Dorset, Vermont

Cover and book design by TH Design, Atlanta, Georgia, thdesign.com

Book Coach: Judith Kolberg, Atlanta, Georgia, squallpress.net

Printed in the United States of America on recycled paper.

Dedication

To my parents, Rita and Wesley Ruland, who raised our family of six children in Sunderland, Vermont. All those chores we were given to do, from picking up sticks to planting five hundred pine seedlings to pulling weeds (the only "perennial" I didn't like in Mom's garden), planted the seeds of my love for the outdoors and gardening.

Also thanks to my husband, Scott, for supporting my hours in the garden as well as in my "office," our kitchen table, filled with the computer, books and papers while I was writing this book.

The illustrations in this book are all drawn by my sister, Kate Ruland, and are dedicated to our maternal grandmother, Katherine Dahl Marino.

Knockout Rose, Shasta Daisy, Veronica, Lamb's Ear, Phlox – Sun

Contents

Welcome

Look out your window and there it is – a perennial garden full of blossoms, buds and greenery. Daisies, iris, ferns, hostas, roses and more; from spring through fall, color and scent to enjoy along with many choices to cut for bouquets.

You have always wanted a perennial garden, but where do you start? This book is written just for you!

Whether you are new to gardening or have a perennial bed that you would like to improve…whether you are busy 24/7 or have time to spare…whether your garden is in containers on a patio or in your back yard…I would like to share over 30 years of experience as a gardener to help you have the perennial garden you have always dreamed of.

This book is full of practical, no-nonsense advice and tips on favorite perennials grown in my gardens. It is an easy-to-read, illustrated guide to reliable choices for both the sun and the shade.

Gardening is a labor of love; it is a joy to the heart and the soul.

Gardening builds friendships; gardeners love to share plants and experience.

Gardening is good for the mind and the body; it relieves stress, burns calories and strengthens your body.

Please enjoy this book as you choose your plants, get your hands in the dirt and grow…

Happy Gardening!

What is a Perennial?

Plants that have a lifespan of more than 2 years.

Perennials are permanent, persistant and returning.

What is an Annual?

Plants that grow and flower in a single season.

Annuals are planted once a year.

Crocosmia, Yarrow, Lamb's Ear – Sun to Part Shade

Garden Design and Planning

As you start exploring the pages of my favorite perennials, here are some basic design concepts to consider for your garden.

Site selection

Match the garden to the size of your yard or property, as well as your amount of leisure time.

Choose a space to showcase and view the perennials from the inside of your home as well as the outside areas.

Styles of Gardens

There are many ways to use perennials in a garden design. The preferred style is all a matter of taste.

Formal: usually involves a structure such as a wall, fence or walkway. Balanced and symmetrical with a repetition of size, color and shape. Good proportion and scale according to the house and yard. Accessories are classic – stone urns, cement birdbaths, wrought iron gates – to name a few. Colonial Gardens are this style.

Informal: relaxed and asymmetrically balanced. Loose and colorful, with different textures. Garden art here and there. (Just be careful not to over-power the perennials, which should be the stars of the show!) Cottage Gardens are informal.

It is your garden – don't worry – elements of formal and informal look wonderful together.

Types of Gardens

Choose a garden shape to complement the lawn, any structures, trees and most important, the contours and size of the available land.

Bed: an area of soil prepared for planting.

> *Island Bed*: normally a free-standing, free-form bed of perennials mixed with shrubs under tall trees for a natural setting in an expanse of lawn. A rule of thumb is to place the tallest plants in the center, with the lower growers progressively working out toward the edges.

> *Mixed Border/Bed*: a mixture of perennials, annuals, shrubs and small

trees, whether deciduous or evergreen. Always include flowering shrubs, such as hydrangeas and azaleas, to have interesting year-round combinations. This is my favorite way to design – a casual appearance, an outcome that was not premeditated or fret over!

Perennial Bed: any size garden planted at the edge of the lawn, along a patio or building. Normally filled with a collection of perennials meant to be viewed close-up, therefore should contain plants that keep a neater appearance year-round.

Perennial Border: normally longer than beds, bordering a building, walkway, fence, etc. Usually thought of as the typical English garden, a space to create a lovely and time-consuming garden.

Design

Choose plants with each season in mind or simply, your favorites. Start with perennials with long blooming periods for the most success and enjoyment. The larger the gardens become, the more extensive the wish list of plants will become.

Mix and match the foliage, especially for shady spots. Make sure the texture and color of the leaves and stems is worth viewing all season long.

Use a single plant, known as a specimen, as a punctuation in the garden – where a pop of color, texture or attention is needed.

Color Design

Color is the largest component of any perennial garden – that's usually why we garden!

Choice and combinations of colors are limited only by our imaginations – use nature as the guide. It does not always follow the rule books.

Ideas for successful use of color:

Monochromatic: all shades of a single color.

Warm colors: reds, oranges, yellows make the garden appear closer.

Cool colors: water colors – blues, greens, violets – make the garden recede.

Non-colors: Remember that white and green are also colors!

Variegated foliage is another great way to add color to your garden and brighten up a dark corner at the same time.

Plant Selection

Don't be disappointed if not all your desired plants work in your area; it just doesn't happen sometimes. Check with your local nurseries for a plant similar in characteristics that will grow successfully for you.

When purchasing plants, select full and lush specimens, not necessarily the tallest or in full bloom – better to enjoy the blossoms in your garden than in the nursery pot.

Avoid overgrown and lanky plants, that is unless it is an end of season sale – cut back, plant and wait for next year – always in a gardener's vocabulary!

Plant Placement

Plan on plenty of room for plants to grow – most perennials will at least double in size – as overcrowding causes health problems.

Set plants on the ground in the desired position – step back to take a look – even go in the house and look out the appropriate windows to make sure the placement is correct and pleasing.

If unsure on how to proceed with your dream of a perennial garden, call in a local Garden Designer to help you get started. They have experience with all of the above information and are so worth the investment.

Once you get started with the planning and implementation, beware – gardening usually evolves into hours of labor, such an enjoyable way to spend our time, particularly seeing the garden grow and bloom!

User's Guide

The next nine pages introduce the format this book will use to describe the characteristics and care of each plant featured here. Each entry provides descriptions of that plant's blooms and foliage and requirements including light, water and fertilizer. What is the best use of that specific plant in your yard, what support does it require, what pests threaten it? Plant by plant, this book will guide you through how best to care for your perennials so you will get the most pleasure from growing them – and perhaps sharing them with your fellow gardeners.

Name of Plant

Light requirements
Blossom
Foliage
Approximate mature size
Deciduous or evergreen

A General Description of the Plant: Thoughts about each plant, all of which I have grown in my Atlanta, Georgia, garden over the past 25 years. The majority of these perennials can be grown successfully in other regions of the country with minor adjustments. Check with your local nursery for suggestions on plants with similar characteristics. Wherever you garden, use these tips and suggestions as a guideline, not as hard and fast rules!

Blossom: The size, color and shape of the blossom.

The majority of plants bloom a few weeks, but others bloom a few months.

For many perennials, the plant and blossoms may need more than one season to truly flourish.

Foliage: The size, color, texture and shape of the leaves.

Evergreen: keeps the foliage year round.

Deciduous: loses all of its leaves in the winter.

Light: The requirement of daylight needed for each plant to grow and flourish in the growing season. Below is a guideline explaining light needs listed on plant tags.

Full sun: A minimum of 6 hours of direct sunlight per day.

Full shade: Mostly shaded area with 2 hours or less of direct sun daily. Not many plants produce an abundance of blooms in full shade.

Part shade: More shade than sun. Approximately 3-4 hours of sun per day, basically morning sun.

Part sun: More sun than shade.

Dappled shade: The sunlight that shines through deciduous trees.

Afternoon summer sun (especially in the southern states) is hard on most plants, whatever the conditions!

Water: The water requirements for each plant. This may be the hardest part to explain to gardeners as environmental conditions (sun exposure, wind, soil conditions, tree canopies) vary from garden to garden. Water is an essential element to any garden's success.

Perennials, new or transplanted to the garden, need to be watered deeply immediately after planting.

Before planting, placing the plant for a few minutes in a bucket of water to thoroughly soak the root ball is a great practice for all types of plants – shrubs, perennials and annuals alike.

Rain is always best! The plants just seem to perk up with a good soaking from the sky.

Hand watering with a hose or bucket is the next choice, directing the water into the soil around the roots.

Water carefully (not a hard jet spray) to avoid splattering the dirt onto the foliage.

Soaker hoses placed around the plants' roots work well also but can be unsightly before the foliage covers them – this is a personal choice.

Overhead watering should be done in the morning. The plants will become hydrated in advance of the afternoon sun and dry off before the evening, decreasing the chance of fungus and mildew problems developing.

Evaporation is another reason not to use overhead sprinklers in the heat of the day. The water will vanish before it can soak down into the soil – a waste of water!

Unsure of when to water? The best way to decide is to do the finger test every day or two after planting and weekly during the summer months: feel down around the roots about 3-4" – if it feels moist, no need to water that day.

For the majority of perennials, letting the soil dry out between waterings is better than keeping it constantly wet.

Do not "sprinkle" the garden every day – a good drenching once or twice a week with a hand-held hose is much better for the root system.

Watch for leaf wilt or a fading of green leaves to grayish – a sign the plant is in need of water. However, if a wilted plant does not perk up after a watering, it may be a sign of overwatering and root rot!

For watering new plants the first year, the following is a guideline (every garden has its own environmental issues):

Hot months: 3 times per week

Warm months: 2-3 times per week

Cool months: 2 times per week

Cold months: One time every few weeks, especially with wind and no rainfall

A good investment to keep track of exactly how much rain has fallen is a large, easy-to-read rain gauge placed outside a window in an open area.

When installing an automatic irrigation system, if possible, have separate zones so when watering the lawn, it doesn't water the flower beds also. Established perennials just don't need as much water to keep them hydrated as some lawn grasses do.

In most conditions, an inch of rain per week in the summer months would be a gardener's delight!

Remember, plants in the shade need moisture also! This is especially true if they have competition for water from tree roots – the trees usually win!

Watering in the winter months when perennials are dormant is not necessary or recommended.

Use: Ideas for each plant about where it will look its best and thrive, such as:

Woodland areas
Mixed borders
Mass plantings
Rock gardens
Containers
Mailbox areas
Walkways
Enclosed city gardens
Along a fence/wall

Planting Tips: When and how to plant, addition of soil amendments and the use of mulch.

Most perennials are best planted/transplanted in the fall and, if not, then early spring.

How to Plant: Preparing the soil correctly is the number one step in successful gardening. It will save you time and frustration in the long run.

Not sure of the ultimate size of the plant? It is best to allow at least a 12" space between most perennials.

The majority of perennials do not perform well in wet, poorly-drained soil. If necessary, plant in a raised bed or a bermed area.

Instructions based on a 1 gallon plant

Using a shovel, dig a hole as deep as the size of the pot or the root ball (the depth of the shovel is usually perfect) and at least twice as wide – think of a flat-bottomed hole.

Add amendments to the soil you removed and to the planting hole, making sure the soil is loose. Leaving a bit of clay in the mixture works well for water retention.

Remove the plant from the container carefully – don't tug on the stems. If the roots are tightly wound, gently pull apart or slice into the roots about 1/2" with a garden knife or trowel. Spread the roots out before planting.

Place the plant in the prepared hole, keeping the top of the root ball about 1" higher than the surrounding area.

Fill in the hole around the plant with soil and amendments, making sure the base of the stem is not covered up with soil. Water well!

Mulch the area covering the roots of the plant with the suggestions listed below.

Soil amendments: Materials added to the planting hole to help loosen and aerate the soil as well as to retain moisture.

Examples of soil amendments are Cow/Hen manure, Mushroom Compost, sand, Permatill, your own shredded leaves/compost or bagged soil conditioner such as Nature's Helper. Your local nurseries will have a good selection of products that work well for your type of soil.

Mulch: Any natural material of your choice used as a covering placed around the roots of plants to help shield against temperature changes, control weeds and prevent evaporation of moisture. Next to good soil preparation, mulching is the best practice for growing healthy perennials.

Mulch keeps soil temperature moderate: cooler in summer and warmer in winter. It also prevents soil and nutrients from washing away during hard rains. An added benefit is that as the mulch decomposes, nutrients and organic materials are added to the soil.

Apply a new layer of mulch at least once a year in early spring, making sure it is not piled up around the stems of plants, as this can cause fungus and hide insects. Dig last season's mulch into the soil to increase the nutrient supply.

Availability of the various mulches differs from region to region. Good options to use with perennials include bagged hardwood/pine bark mulch, shredded leaves, baled pine straw (best for a steep slope and also deters slugs), home-grown compost. The choice is yours!

An extra step to keep weeds from sprouting is to place 5-6 newspaper pages down on top of the soil before adding the mulch. Do not use the black weed control fabric – it is very hard to dig through, and over time, soil builds up on it and weeds grow on top! I also do not recommend use of rubber mulch or white or red small rocks as mulch for perennials – these draw in heat and do not provide any nutrients whatsoever!

Fertilizer: Chemical or natural (organic) products added to the soil that aid in providing nutrients to the plant.

Preference of chemical or organic fertilizer in your garden is truly a personal choice. Going green by using organic products is always a good thing!

The following is a quick and simple explanation of the numbers found on the containers of fertilizer, e.g., 10-10-10:

1st number: Nitrogen – promotes leaf growth.

2nd number: Phosphorous – promotes the roots and formation of flower growth.

3rd number: Potassium – overall health.

It is advantageous to have your soil tested by the local Extension Service for these minerals and other necessary nutrients.

Chemical: 10-10-10 pellets are a common all-purpose fertilizer.

Osmocote or a similar brand is a time-released fertilizer that releases nutrients for a few months when watered.

Granular products, such as Miracle Gro, are mixed with water for a short-term fertilizer that is good during the summer for a quick pick-me-up every couple of weeks. This method is also known as foliar feeding – a gentle spray on the leaves, best applied on a cloudy day. This is especially helpful if a lot of rain has washed the spring fertilizer away or in regions with a long growing season.

At planting/transplanting time, using a liquid product such as Upstart mixed with water encourages the root system to develop. Also useful when planting any type of plants in containers. Follow directions on the label.

Organic: Any type of composted material of your own making or purchased commercial items such as Holly Tone, Milorganite, Bone Meal, Blood Meal, Cottonseed Meal, etc. Fresh manures need to be composted for a few months as seeds may be present, depending on what the animal feasted on!

Covering the soil surrounding the plant with a compost of your choice is a very beneficial practice to grow healthy plants – compost is considered to be one of the best fertilizers for perennials.

A few reminders

Fertilizer should be added only when the plant is in its growing season. Scattering the fertilizer around the plants should be done in early spring as the soil temperature begins to warm up.

Do not apply any additional nutrients after blooms diminish. Let them prepare to go dormant.

It is difficult to harm a plant by giving it the wrong fertilizer, just never use a lawn fertilizer!

Whatever fertilizer you choose, just don't overdo it or put it directly on the stem base, especially in the heat of summer – I've done it, burned the plant, not pretty!!

Plant Support: Certain plants may need to be staked or tied up to keep them from falling over in the wind and rain, or simply because they become overly large as the season progresses and blossoms weigh them down.

Plants tend to lean toward the sun and may shade neighboring plants.

A few of the many options for support that are available: string and bamboo stakes, single-wire loops, wire rings, tomato cages. You can always make your own from sturdy twigs!

Place the ring or hoop over the plant when it is small – this will keep the plant from breaking if you try to put it on when it is full grown – believe me, I've tried, and it was not a good result!

Pruning: A majority of perennials should be pruned back at the beginning of the growing season to produce stocky, sturdier stems and a more compact plant. This is known as the "Chelsea Chop." (In England this practice is done around the time of the Chelsea Flower Show.) Once the plant is about half the full-grown size, remove approximately one-third of the plant with hand pruners. This practice will delay the blooms by a couple of weeks, but the stronger stems will help to prevent the plant from falling over due to the weight of the blossoms later in the season.

Most plants should be dead-headed during the blooming season – with pruners, remove old blooms, including some with the complete stems to encourage new growth.

Each perennial listed in this book will have its own schedule of when and how to prune throughout the season. At the end of the season, most perennials should be trimmed back, leaving a few inches of stems or the ground hugging leaves at the base.

Placing a plant identification stake in the ground will help identify the location of plants once they have gone dormant for the winter. This answers the question for many gardeners, "What in the world did I plant in that spot?!"

There are many types of pruning shears available – find one that fits your hand nicely and doesn't cause strain on your wrists and elbows.

Tying a brightly-colored ribbon on pruners (especially if they are dark in color!) makes it much easier to find them when they are left in the garden – somewhere!

Dividing/Sharing: Most plants need to be divided every few years or moved to a different site after a season or two (and then maybe again!!) to maintain a healthy root system.

The best time to do this chore is in the morning on an overcast day when the plants are still full of moisture.

Use a shovel or hand trowel to dig the plant out of the ground, taking as much of the root ball as possible.

To divide a plant, cut into sections with a garden knife or pull apart gently with your hands, depending on the type of root system. Discard any dried up or infected sections.

Replant as soon as possible in newly amended soil and water.

For sharing with a fellow gardener (we are a generous group and love to share), a plastic grocery bag is the perfect place to store most plants for a short period. Write the name of the plant on it and add water.

Placing an open umbrella over a new plant is a good way to protect a transplant from the hot sun for the first few days.

Pests/Problems: Solutions on coping with insects and wildlife, along with various plant diseases. Please control the use of overall chemical spraying, as this kills the good as well as the bad insects.

Many new products are available as a systemic control – absorbed through the roots, the product goes up through the stems and is effective for many months. The best part: there is no spraying involved, therefore it doesn't harm birds or beneficial insects.

Most insects that visit perennials can be dealt with by a quick spray of the hose. Additional solutions for a few of the pesky problems:

Aphids: Plant lice. Those 1/4" long, soft-bodied insects that cluster on new plant growth and suck the juices, leaving a sticky residue that can become sooty mold. Control with insecticidal soap (five or six drops of liquid dish soap in a quart of water). Use a spray bottle to mist both top and bottom of leaves every 2-3 days for a couple of weeks. Prepared commercial products are available at your local nursery or hardware store.

Black spot and powdery mildew: For prevention, give plants sufficient light and air circulation. Pick off and destroy infected foliage and flowers. Spray with a horticultural oil, or use a systemic product following label directions.

Root rot: Provide excellent drainage, especially in the winter. If necessary, use a copper-based fungicide.

Slugs: Slimy little creatures that eat leaves and flowers, leaving behind a trail of slime. To rid the garden of these pests, keep the garden free of debris in which they hide and breed. An iron-phosphate product works well to kill them as does using a hollowed-out half of a cantaloupe turned face down – check every couple days to see how many have crawled in, and discard the varmints!

Deer and rabbits: To control, use fences, chicken wire, motion-detector water sprinklers, or products such as Deer-Off and Blood Meal.

Cut Flowers: For the most part, the perennials listed are ideal to cut for use in a bouquet or arrangement, small or large. Here are a few suggestions:

Cut the blossoms in the morning or evening (always a debate on this), but not in the middle of the day.

Choose blossoms that are not quite yet in full bloom – they will last longer.

With pruning shears or scissors, cut the stem cleanly – don't break it off.

Carry a bucket of warm water with you and immediately place the stems in it – don't let them lie in the sun on the ground while you do another chore!

Strip all the lower leaves and buds off to prevent disease in the vase.

Trim the stems once again on a slant before arranging.

Zones: The United States is divided into Plant Hardiness Zones by the USDA, ranging from Zone 2, the coldest, to Zone 10, the hottest. These are the expected minimum temperatures in which plants will survive.

For example, Bleeding Heart is listed on page 37 to grow in Zones 3-7. This means that the plant will survive the average low winter temperatures of Zone 3, but that it will also grow fairly well in zones up to at least the cooler parts of Zone 7.

Environmental variables in each region such as unusually hot or cold winters, rainfall, wind, etc., can affect the plants' growing conditions as well as the placement in your own backyard!

Additional or Favorite Varieties: A list of varieties that are available – by no means a complete list!

Gardener's Notes: Use this section to make notes for each plant:

Spring arrival
Blooming period
Pruning time
Problems or pests
Success or failure
Where dormant perennials are planted
New varieties to try
Maintenance schedule
Chores to do next season – divide, move, buy more!

Ajuga

Full sun to part shade
Blue/purple blossom
Green or purple foliage
4-10"t x 1'w
Deciduous

Ajuga reptans is a very effective ground cover for part shade areas, with the foliage being the main event. It spreads (some say too much – not me!) by runners, forming a mat that thrives in locations dreaded by most other plants, such as dry shade beneath trees.

Blossom: Blue 3-5" tall spikes bloom on most varieties, anywhere from late spring to early fall. Planted in a mass, it becomes a showy spectacle when in full bloom.

Foliage: Glossy and oval, the spinach-like leaves are 2-4" long. Colors range from dark green to a tri-color of green, plum and brown. The variegated forms tend to be less vigorous, useful for small areas.

Light: Part shade to shade, depending on the moisture.

Water: With good drainage, regular watering is best. This plant is fairly drought tolerant.

Use: Valuable as a solid weed-proof groundcover, as an edging, or in containers. Also attractive in groupings of 3-5 in front of short chartreuse or black grasses, hostas, ferns or low-growing evergreen shrubs.

Planting Tips: Place 6"-1' apart in areas with excellent drainage and air circulation to help prevent crown/root rot. Average to rich soil will encourage the plant to multiply, if so desired. When planted on the edge of a bed near a lawn, allow for some room to spread. However, it is an easy plant to keep in check by pulling/digging away the runners. Best planted in spring or early fall.

Fertilizer: Not necessary, but a time-released fertilizer can be used each spring.

Pruning: Trim off or dig away wayward runners if needed to keep in check. The blossoms will dry up after blooming or can be snipped off.

Dividing/Sharing: Easy to dig out a portion of the plant to divide or share – best done in early spring or fall.

Pests/Problems: Problems are usually associated with too much moisture and humidity. If crown rot appears, just remove the infected portion.

Cut Flower: Try a few in a small vase or mixed bouquet!

Zones: 3-9

Recommended Varieties: All produce blue/purple blossoms.
   Black Scallop – burgundy foliage, 3-6"
   Burgundy Glow – multi-colored foliage, 3-6"
   Caitlin's Giant – bronze foliage, 10-15"
   Chocolate Chip – bronze foliage, 2-3"
   Dixie Chip – tri-colored foliage, 3-6"

Gardener's Notes:

_____

_____

_____

_____

Ajuga, Iris, Brown-Eyed Susan – Sun

Artemisia

Full sun
Silver-grey foliage
No blooms
2-3't x 3'w
Evergreen/Deciduous

Powis Castle seems to be the best choice of the Artemisias, especially for regions with hot, humid summers. This fast grower is chosen by gardeners for the silver-grey foliage that adds a calming feeling to the garden.

Blossom: Will sprout a small yellow flower if not pruned regularly. Grown for the foliage, not the blossom!

Foliage: The fern-like leaves have a nice silver-grey color, lending an excellent contrast to brightly colored flowers or dark green foliage. Very aromatic when touched.

Light: Full sun.

Water: It will tolerate poor, dry conditions but performs best with regular watering. The worst condition for Artemisia is wet feet, especially in the winter!

Use: Fantastic as a filler plant to cover the bare legs of taller plants in late summer. Great at a gate or walkway entrance, giving off a pleasant aroma as people walk by. Powis Castle also works well in the mixed garden to soften reds and oranges and blends well with pinks, blues and lavenders. Shows up nicely against a green foliage background as well as a dark wall or fence. Combine with other drought-tolerant sun lovers in containers for an outstanding display.

Planting Tips: Plant in loose, well-drained soil in a slightly elevated area to provide excellent drainage. Spring is the best time to plant as the soil warms up allowing the root system to grow. Provide plenty of room as it will grow 2-3' tall and wide quickly.

Fertilizer: This plant does not need to be fertilized annually; a top dressing of compost will suffice.

Plant Support: If planted in a shady spot, it will become leggy and need to be staked. Can also be planted behind low growers to provide support as it leans forward.

Pruning: To keep a nice round shape and encourage fresh growth, prune back in mid-spring to about 12" when new growth appears – never prune in the fall. Throughout the growing season, remove about 2-3" of the stem tips every month. This will result in a more lush, less woody plant, which helps to prevent it from opening up in the center and flopping over.

Dividing/Sharing: Artemisia does not really spread or multiply because of its woody nature. To transplant, do so in late winter or early spring.

Pests/Problems: Root rot will occur from too much moisture, especially in winter. Aphids may be a problem; use insecticidal soap spray. Seldom bothered by deer.

Cut Flower: It doesn't seem to work for me – it wilts, even though the color would be a great addition to a vase!

Zones: 5-8

Gardener's Notes:

_____

_____

_____

_____

Aster

Full sun to part shade

Pink, purple, white or blue blooms

Small, medium green leaves

6"-4⁺'t x 2-4'w

Deciduous

Asters add a much-needed burst of color to the garden in the fall when many perennials' and annuals' blooms are declining. It is a very tough plant that is available in many colors and sizes. Definitely worth the wait for the fall blooms – even though the plant may look a bit weedy in the summer.

Blossom: A daisy-like bloom in shades of pink, blue, purple or white, with a yellow or purple center. The blossom can be single, semi-double or double and is very persistent in its flowering.

Foliage: The leaves are small, lance shaped and usually smooth edged.

Light: Full sun to part shade, happy with afternoon shade in very hot areas.

Water: Evenly moist soil is best, but it can take some drought with weekly watering in mid-summer. Asters are tolerant of wet soil.

Use: The shorter Aster looks great in a group that can form a mass of blossoms in the front of the garden while the taller varieties definitely need to be in the back section. Surround them with other sun-loving plants to disguise their sometimes weedy appearance before bloom time. Mix with Goldenrod, Ornamental Grasses and other Asters for a great fall garden. Also, very showy as a container plant – replace worn out summer bloomers with an Aster!

Planting Tips: Amend the soil with lots of compost. Mulch to keep the roots cool in the summer. Space the plants at about half their full-grown height to provide good air circulation.

Fertilizer: Each spring and fall, top-dress with cow manure or a similar product containing organic matter.

Plant Support: The taller varieties definitely need staking to prevent the stems from breaking during a storm. A large hoop/tomato cage-type stake works well as long as it is put on early in the season before the plant gets too tall.

Pruning: Asters respond well to trimming back by at least one-third in late spring to early summer. This practice helps to prevent leggy plants and makes for a tidy, sturdier plant. Remove the stems down to ground level after the blossoms have faded.

Dividing/Sharing: In early spring or late fall, Asters can be divided by digging up the entire clump and separating with a shovel or garden knife. Usually, the center becomes weak and should be discarded; replant the vigorous outer sections. Do this every 2-3 years for healthy plants.

Attracts: Butterflies and bees.

Pests/Problems: Powdery mildew and aphids can be a problem – control with an insecticidal soap spray. Rabbits love to nibble on Asters!

Cut Flower: All varieties are wonderful to use in arrangements. Change the water daily.

Zones: 3-9

Favorite Varieties:
Alma Potschke – salmon pink, 3'
Fanny – blue, 24"
Harrington's Pink – 3-5'
Hella Lacy – purple, 3-4'
Purple Dome – 18-24"
Raydon's Favorite – blue, 3-4'
Tatarian – light lavender, 7'
Wood's Blue, Purple & Pink – 9-12"

Gardener's Notes:

Asteromoea mongolica   Mongolian aster

Aster – Ghenghis Kahn

Full sun to part shade
Small white blooms
Feathery green leaves
18-24"t x 24+"w
Deciduous

Ghenghis Kahn Aster is one of my favorite perennials. Not as over-powering as its name, the dainty daisy-like bloom begins in May on 18-24" stem and continues on into the fall. I have it in both full sun and part shade – where it has adapted and starts blooming a week or so later than the plant in full sun.

Blossom: The blooms are less than 1" round with white petals and a yellow center. They appear all over the multi-stemmed plant.

Foliage: The medium green leaves are a couple inches long and slender, with a fern-like appearance. Multiple stems come off the main stem, giving a bushy and full appearance.

Light: Full sun to part shade.

Water: Can tolerate some temporary drought, but does best with a weekly watering of about 1".

Use: Plant this Aster where it can spread to at least 3' in width. Because of the small bloom, you will enjoy it more after a couple seasons when it grows into a nice, large clump. Spreads, but is not invasive. Great as a filler plant in many areas of the garden.

Planting Tips: Added amendments will reward you with fuller plants; however, it can tolerate poor soil.

Fertilizer: Use 10-10-10 or a time-released product such as Osmocote every spring. Liquid fertilizer in the summer will help it thrive and continue to bloom into the fall.

Plant Support: When planted in more shade, it may get leggier and need some type of staking. If it is planted behind a sturdier plant, such as Black-Eyed Susan, it will be fine.

Pruning: Prune this perennial during the growing season at least twice. In early spring when it reaches about 18", take off about a third to prevent it from becoming too leggy for the summer. Early to mid-August, trim about one-third off to remove old blooms and stems. This seems to rejuvenate it to continue blooming until mid-fall.

Dividing/Sharing: Very easy to dig up portions with a shovel to divide in either spring or fall – your friends will be thankful for this plant!

Pests/Problems: None noticed.

Cut Flower: Looks best in small vases. There are many blooms on each stem, but they do tend to fade quickly.

Zones: 3-8

Gardener's Notes:

_____

_____

_____

_____

_____

_____

TIP
Carry a 5-gallon bucket or
lightweight container around with
you to throw debris, weeds, etc. in.

Astilbe

Partial shade
Variety of bloom colors
Medium green ferny leaves
2-3't x 2'w
Deciduous

Astilbe does well in the partial-shade garden, with a very airy, pretty bloom that rises gracefully above the fern-like foliage on a wiry stem in late spring. A good long-lasting plant – some of mine are over 25 years old!

Bloom: Feathery, arching spikes, 6-10" tall x 3-4" wide, appear in late spring in a range of colors from white to red to peach.

Foliage: Fern-like medium green leaves completely die back in the winter but are very appealing all summer even after the blooms have faded. The foliage, if kept moist, forms an attractive groundcover.

Light: Partial shade, needs some early-morning sun. Does not bloom well in deep, full shade.

Water: Needs to stay moist, especially in half-day sun, but does not like not soggy feet either. If this plant dries out, the foliage will turn brown and disappear for the remainder of a dry season.

Use: Perfect to mix among Ferns, Hostas, Solomon's Seal and other morning sun lovers. Looks best planted in groups of at least three plants so their blooms make more of a statement. Mixing the colors together is striking. Looks very natural along a creek bed or pond as long as its roots are not submerged in the water.

Planting Tips: Add plenty of organic matter to the planting area – shredded leaves, mushroom compost, etc. – to keep the soil around the roots evenly moist. Mulch is necessary.

Fertilizer: Heavy feeders. Add a slow-release fertilizer at planting time and sprinkle around the plant each spring. A liquid mixture, such as

Miracle Gro, during the season is helpful. Top-dress with compost every spring.

Plant Support: A single loop stake might be needed for the bloom when it gets full, as the rain may weigh it down.

Pruning: Trim off old blooms at base of stem as they turn brown to keep a tidy appearance. Remove all foliage once frost hits or when the plant becomes brown during a drought.

Dividing/Sharing: Divide the plants in early spring once they sprout up a few inches or in late fall. To ensure the plants' vigor, divide every 3-4 years and replant in rich soil.

Attracts: Butterflies and bees.

Pests/Problems: None, except prolonged drought!

Cut Flower: Very nice, but I find it hard to remove the blossoms from the plant – they look so beautiful out in the garden!

Zones: 4-8

Favorite Varieties:
  Bridal Veil – white
  Fanal – red
  Rhineland – pink

Gardener's Notes:

_____

_____

_____

_____

_____

_____

Astilbe – Chinese

Partial shade
Purplish-pink plumes
Fern-like foliage
1-2't x 2'w
Deciduous

Chinese Astilbe var. Pumila has creeping foliage that grows about 6+" tall with very erect 10-12" tall purple-pink fuzzy plumes, blooming early to mid summer. A very reliable variety of Astilbe and a low-maintenance perennial for the part-shade garden area.

Blossom: Purple-pink plumes, about 10-12" tall and 2" wide, appear on sturdy stems in early summer. The color will fade, leaving an interesting texture for the remainder of the season.

Foliage: Medium green fern-like leaves grow about 5-6" long.

Light: Chinese Astilbe can tolerate more sun than the arendsii variety. Morning sun with afternoon shade is ideal.

Water: Regular watering is best to achieve full plants. If the leaves curl and become brown on the edges, the plants need more moisture and, most likely, less sun. That said, this variety can withstand temporary drought.

Use: Because of its adaptability to different environments, this plant can be used in bog gardens and other areas with less than ideal water conditions. Looks nice placed in front of taller plants such as hostas, ferns, or any morning sun lover. Using five or more plants together makes a nice groundcover.

Planting Tips: Work lots of compost/organic matter into the soil to achieve a very fertile, loose planting area. Mulch with chopped leaves, shredded bark, etc., to retain moisture.

Fertilizer: At planting time, as well as every spring, cover the planted area with compost to provide a natural fertilizer.

Pruning: Trim off old blooms at the base (or leave for a natural look), and remove all foliage before frost.

Dividing/Sharing: To keep plants vigorous, dig up and divide every 3-4 years in the spring or fall – a perfect time to share this beauty with fellow gardeners.

Pests/Problems: None noticed, except finding the correct moisture to make it happy.

Cut Flower: Flower arrangements will benefit from the fuzzy texture of the plumes.

Zones: 3-8

Additional Varieties:
    Finale – pale rose-pink
    Intermezzo – salmon-pink
    Serenade – rose-red

Gardener's Notes:

_____

_____

_____

_____

Autumn Fern

Partial to full shade
No blooms
Green/copper foliage
24-30"t x 18-24"w
Evergreen

Autumn Fern is the most popular evergreen fern for many reasons – it is very hardy, adaptable, fairly drought tolerant and adds a cool, airy feel to shady spots as well as containers.

Foliage: One of the few ferns to provide seasonal color with beautiful coppery/orange new growth in the spring. By summer, the fronds (fern foliage) become a glossy green color. A two- to three-year-old plant will grow into a clump 24-30" tall by 24" wide.

Light: Partial to full shade. Can take some morning sun, but in summer, afternoon sun will scorch the foliage.

Water: Regular watering is best to provide moist soil rewarding you with full, lush plants. That said, Autumn Ferns seem to survive just fine in temporary drought conditions in the shade.

Use: Planted in the middle to back of the garden or as a foundation plant, groups of three to five are great for a mass planting. Autumn Fern makes a statement as a single plant given plenty of room to show off its beautiful fronds. Among boulders, along a stream bed, near a gate or against the shady side of a mailbox – all are perfect settings for this fern.

Containers: For winter containers in mild areas, Autumn Fern is a great choice. It can take almost full sun, mixed with other plants such as Heucheras and Pansies. When spring arrives, along with the colorful new growth, remove from the container and plant in a partial shade area in the garden. For summer containers, it is perfect mixed with Dragon Wing Begonias, Impatiens, Torenias and other shade lovers.

Planting Tips: As for all ferns, it is best to dig a hole much wider than deep – think of a flat-bottomed bowl. The crown (top of root ball) should never be below the soil surface. Add a few shovelfuls of composted leaves or bagged manure/soil conditioner to the hole. Water every day for a week or two to help set the root ball in. Add mulch around the base.

Fertilizer: Every spring, as the fronds start popping out of the ground, cover the area with a layer of compost.

Plant Support: Use green bamboo or metal stakes to hold up fronds if they are leaning over a neighboring plant – as well as to keep a natural arching look.

Pruning: In early spring, cut off any fronds at the soil line that have turned brown, broken or are lying on the ground, being careful not to snip the unfurling new fronds. Throughout the season, trim away any fronds as needed to keep the garden tidy.

Dividing/Sharing: Easy to transplant or divide as the root ball is not very large. Best done in early spring or late fall. Remember to amend the soil in the new location.

Pests/Problems: None, not even deer!

Cut Flower: A nice foliage addition to an arrangement. Cut off at the soil line and remove a few of the lower leaves before adding to your vase.

Zones: 5-9

Gardener's Notes:

_____

_____

_____

_____

_____

_____

Blackberry Lily

Full sun to part shade

Yellow, apricot, orange-red blooms

Green sword-shaped leaves

2-3't x 1'w

Deciduous

Blackberry Lily is an easy-to-grow plant, some say too easy in that it will self sow here and there! It is a relative of the Iris, with very similar leaves. In the summer as well as fall, it adds texture and an interesting look to the perennial garden. The plants form a clump of foliage about 1-2' tall x 8-12" wide, and the flower stems rise above at about 24" tall.

Blossom: Each bloom is made up of 6 petals, 1-2" wide, rising on stems above the foliage. Colors range from cream to yellow to apricot, with darker spotting. Blooms from July to September. In the fall following the flower, a beige seed capsule opens to reveal a shiny blackberry-like seed pod, therefore the name.

Foliage: Medium green sword-shaped leaves form a clump 18-36" tall and 12" wide, depending on the variety.

Light: Grows fine in full sun but can also take a few hours of shade.

Water: Regular watering is best, but Blackberry Lily is fairly drought resistant.

Use: Very appealing in a mass planting of at least five to seven plants or scattered here and there to fill in gaps. Also perfect in containers for additional texture and height.

Planting Tips: The roots are a small rhizome (tube) that should be planted only 1" deep and 1' apart. They are not particular about the soil, as they sprout up here and there from the seed pods.

Fertilizer: 10-10-10 or a time-released fertilizer scattered over the soil when the foliage appears in the spring.

Plant support: A small, single-ring support is helpful for top-heavy plants once the blooming begins, especially in part shade.

Pruning: Cut off the stem at the base in the late fall/winter.

Dividing/Sharing: Once you have this plant, it will appear (aka volunteers) in late spring/early summer all around the garden. The plants are very easy to pop out of the ground with a trowel and move to another spot, add to existing plants to make more of a mass planting, use in a container or just give away. Dividing an existing clump is a simple chore with a shovel.

Pests/Problems: To control possible Iris borers, keep the area free of dying leaves, etc., that cover the rhizomes (roots).

Cut Flower: Does very well in a vase by itself with the foliage or in a mixed bouquet. The seed pods look great in fall arrangements for a contrasting texture.

Zones: 4-10

Favorite Varieties:

    May be listed as either 'chinensis' or 'flabellata'
    Hello Yellow – buttery yellow blooms, 1.5'
    Freckle Face – apricot with red spots, 2-3'

Gardener's Notes:

_____

_____

_____

_____

_____

_____

_____

Late season surprise

Black-Eyed Susan

Full sun to part shade
Yellow daisy-like bloom
Dark green foliage
24-36"t and spreads
Deciduous

Black-Eyed Susan is the workhorse of any summer garden adding bright, long-lasting color from early July into September. Goldsturm is an excellent variety, growing 24-36" tall and spreading into a broad clump, but it doesn't take over the garden.

Blossom: A daisy-looking bloom, with deep yellow petals and a dark brown/black center, about 2" round.

Foliage: The dark green leaves are thin and oval shaped with a hairy, rough feeling.

Light: Full sun to part shade.

Water: Regular watering is helpful, but Black-Eyed Susan is fairly drought tolerant once established.

Use: Goldsturm is great in so many places – a grouping in the perennial bed, a couple of plants by the mailbox, a few along the front sidewalk in front of shrubbery as well as in a large container on the deck. Try planting with sun-tolerant ferns (Southern Shield) – a great combination!

Planting Tips: Amended, well-drained soil will give the best results. Mulch to retain moisture.

Fertilizer: Scatter a time-released fertilizer such as Osmocote around the plant each spring as well as a layer of compost of your choice to add nutrients to the soil.

Plant Support: May need some staking, especially if growing in partial shade.

Pruning: Trim off spent blooms along with the stem, down to the next leaf and bud, as this encourages more blooms. If you can tolerate the spent look, leave several stems as birds love to snack on the seeds in the center cones. Mid to late fall is the time to trim stems down to the ground, leaving the bottom foliage.

Dividing/Sharing: Divide at least every 3-4 years – dig up the clump and separate into sections. Plant in new garden spots or share with friends.

Attracts: Butterflies and bees enjoy the blossoms, and goldfinches love the remaining seed pods.

Pests/Problems: Aphids may bother them as well as little black beetles that occupy the center of the bud. Treat both by spraying the whole plant with an insecticidal soap early in the season every few days for a couple of weeks.

Cut Flower: A great addition to the summer bouquet or looks pretty in a vase all by itself. Very long-lasting, especially when the water is changed every couple of days.

Zones: 3-8

Gardener's Notes:

_____

_____

_____

_____

Bleeding Heart - Fernleaf

Part shade
Rosy-pink blooms
Blue-green lacy fronds
1.5't x 1.5'w
Deciduous

Fernleaf Bleeding Heart is a delicate-looking little plant but is much more hardy than it appears. It is a long-lasting bloomer adding a beautiful foliage texture to the shade garden.

Blossom: Rosy/red/pink pendant heart-shaped groups of blooms grow on the tips of the fleshy stems. Blooming begins in late spring and can continue into the fall with adequate moisture.

Foliage: The foliage has a very nice blue-green coloring, with an airy fern-like appearance. Clump forming.

Light: Morning sun with afternoon shade.

Water: Continual slightly moist soil is best; very wet feet will cause root rot, and drought will cause a slow death!

Use: This Bleeding Heart is a nice addition to the front area of the garden to view close up, surrounded by ferns, hostas, or impatiens. Especially striking against burgundy foliage such as Heucheras or purple Oxalis.

Planting Tips: Loosen the soil well and add lots of compost/amendments – will not survive in heavy clay soil. Do not plant too deeply.

Fertilizer: Rich compost spread over the plant roots every spring provides plenty of nutrients.

Plant support: None is needed.

Pruning: Trim back the bloom spikes to the ground after they fade to encourage new blooms. Remove any foliage that yellows during the season. In late fall, trim the whole plant down to the ground.

Dividing/Sharing: Best not to disturb, but if they outgrow their site, or die out in the center with age, dig up and divide in early spring. This plant reproduces by self-sowing.

Pests/Problems: Root rot from too much moisture and poor drainage. Deer resistant.

Cut Flower: The blooms are a sweet addition to any vase, and the foliage lasts even longer. It is very airy, adding a nice texture to any small arrangement.

Zones: 3-8

Additional Varieties:

    Burning Hearts – rosy red flowers outlined with white edges
    Alba – greenish white blooms

Gardener's Notes:

_____

_____

_____

_____

TIP
Put lotion on before your garden gloves to keep your hands moist.

Stick your fingernails in soap before working in the garden so the dirt will wash out more easily!

Bleeding Heart – Old Fashioned

Full to part shade
Feathery leaves
Pink/White Blooms
24-36"t x 18-24"w
Deciduous

Old Fashioned Bleeding Heart is a wonderful shade plant for the early-mid spring garden. The heart-shaped blooms dangle from arching stems, giving a very graceful feel. I just wish it bloomed all year!

Blossom: The heart-shaped 1.5" long blooms are pink and white – so pretty in the shade garden, blooming from April through May.

Foliage: The medium green leaves have a feathery appearance. Once the summer weather begins in hot climates, this Bleeding Heart completely disappears until next spring, but is always worth the wait to see it again.

Light: Full to part shade. Does not do well with afternoon sun.

Water: Continually moist soil is good. Does not like wet feet as this will cause the roots to rot.

Use: Because of its early blooming period, this Bleeding Heart is great in a spot where summer shade annuals (Impatiens, Coleus) can be planted over top. Plant it with Hostas, Ferns, and Solomon's Seal in a woodland setting, against a fence/wall or in any dark, shady spot that needs a pop of color.

Planting Tips: Plant in a rich, amended soil that is well drained. A slight slope is great and you will be rewarded with a very long-lasting beauty. Mulch.

Fertilizer: Add compost to the planting hole as well as around the new sprouts early spring every year.

Plant Support: None – even though the stems are fleshy, they do not bend or break once the blossoms appear.

Pruning: As the blooming begins, trim off any leaves that hide the beautiful little hearts! When the show of blooms is finished and the foliage begins to turn yellow, trim off the stems to the ground.

Dividing/Sharing: It is best to leave undisturbed. However, if necessary because of encroachment from neighboring plants, it can be dug up and moved in the early spring when the new growth appears.

Pests: Fungus caused from root rot. Deer resistant.

Cut Flower: A stem with the little hearts is so sweet in a small bouquet or even by itself in a vase on the windowsill – lasts much longer than you would think!

Zones: 3-7

Additional Varieties:

  Alba – white blooms
  Gold Heart – bright golden leaves

Gardener's Notes:

_____

_____

_____

_____

Blue Fescue Grass

Full sun to part shade
Tan-colored plume
Steely blue foliage
8-12"t x 10-12"w
Evergreen

Blue Fescue is a small, hardy ornamental grass. Add the Elijah Blue variety to your landscape for a unique color and texture. It forms a compact mound that blends well with many types of plants – an eye-catcher all year long.

Blossom: Small tan-colored spikes rise above the foliage in early summer.

Foliage: Fine textured grass, with a vibrant blue-green color.

Light: Full sun to part shade, especially in hot, humid areas.

Water: Very drought tolerant. Let grasses dry out between waterings. In regions with wet summers, it needs excellent drainage, preferably on a slope.

Use: Plant in groups of at least three in the front area of a garden, nestled up against rocks, near evergreens, or as a companion for Lamb's Ear, Variegated Tall Sedum or other plants with low moisture needs. Adds a pretty texture to a container planting.

Planting Tips: Prepare the planting hole with soil conditioner and coarse sand to aid drainage. Make sure it is not planted in a low, soggy area. Provide plenty of space for good air circulation.

Fertilizer: Good soil preparation should provide enough nutrients, but always good to toss a bit of time-released fertilizer around the plants each spring. Not too much mulch close to the base.

Plant Support: None needed.

Pruning: Shear back to 3-4" in the early spring. During the season, using a small metal rake is an easy way to clean out faded foliage.

Dividing/Sharing: To keep the plant vigorous, every three years, dig up and divide the root ball with a serrated knife.

Pests/Problems: Deer resistant, but rabbits seem to enjoy it! After five or more years, some plants tend to die out.

Cut Flower: The tan spikes are perfect for small arrangements.

Zones: 1-9

Additional Variety:

Siskiyou Blue – luminous blue foliage, 1-2' tall

Gardener's Notes:

_____

_____

_____

_____

Black Eyed Susan, Butterfly Weed, Artemisia, Ajuga, Crocosmia, Sedum, Aster – Sun

Brown-Eyed Susan

Full sun
Yellow daisy-like bloom
Medium green foliage
3-4't x 2'w
Deciduous

Triloba is a tall variety of Rudbeckia, a very tough but pleasing group of plants. By the second season, a large single clump over 3' in height produces literally hundreds of flowers on multi-branched stiff stems. The only drawback (not to me!) is the self-seeding that may occur – however, the seedlings are very easy to pull up or transplant to new areas!

Blossom: Often called Brown-Eyed Susan because of the medium brown center, the blooms are small and dainty with yellow petals surrounding the domed center. The blooming period lasts for a couple of months in mid-late summer into the fall.

Foliage: The leaves at the base have three lobes, thus the name. The remainder of the plant's leaves are about 5" long and slender, and medium green.

Light: Full sun, loves warm temperatures.

Water: Fairly drought tolerant, but regular watering and good drainage will reward you with a colorful display for the late summer garden.

Use: Because of Triloba's height, it should be planted in the back of the garden. Looks great in a grouping as a backdrop with shorter plants in front such as Fall Asters or Veronicas. Also pretty grown as a single specimen in a mixed bed, near a garden gate or a mailbox.

Planting Tips: Give this plant a loose, amended soil to grow in, and it will thrive. Mulch to keep roots cool.

Fertilizer: Compost used as mulch should provide plenty of nutrients, but any organic or chemical fertilizer scattered over the soil in the spring is fine.

Plant Support: Triloba benefits from a large tomato cage placed over the plant when it gets to 18" tall, as this will keep it upright once it is loaded with blooms. Planting it near sturdy evergreen shrubs also serves as a brace.

Pruning: A good candidate for the "Chelsea Chop" – when the plant is about 2' tall, trim off about 1' to produce a sturdier specimen. Remove spent blooms throughout the season to encourage blooming into the fall. Trim back to the ground before the first frost, leaving the green leaves at the base.

Dividing/Sharing: Will reseed itself here and there! Simply dig up the new plant, move it to the desired location or give away to a fellow gardener. (Thanks for mine, Ginger!)

Attracts: Bees, butterflies and birds (especially Goldfinch).

Pest/Problems: Occasional aphids and little black beetles can be controlled with an insecticidal soap. Mature plants may only last two to three years, but there is always the new seedling to take their place.

Cut Flower: Forever a favorite in mixed bouquets – or the stems full of yellow blossoms are charming in a vase by themselves.

Zones: 4-10

Gardener's Notes:

_____

_____

_____

_____

> *Earth laughs in flowers.*
> *– Ralph Waldo Emerson*

Butterfly Weed

Full sun
Orange-red blossom
Lance-shaped green leaves
2-3't x 2'w
Deciduous

Butterfly Weed comes by its name naturally. The foliage is an important food source for Monarch Butterfly larvae (caterpillars), and the colorful summer blooms attract many types of butterflies. This tough variety is not a weed, but a showy and easy-to-grow perennial choice for the flower garden. Just don't be upset when the caterpillars start to munch on the foliage – the blossoms and soon-to-appear butterflies are worth the temporary sparseness.

Blossom: Orange-red star-like flowers in clusters atop sturdy stems in early to late summer.

Foliage: 3" long, thin leaves.

Light: Full sun, enjoys the heat.

Water: Moderate water, provide good drainage.

Use: Best planted in the middle to back of the garden with fuller plants in front to cover its leggy nature late in the season. Not suited for planting near a doorway for a close-up view – the foilage may be gone by the end of the season due to the caterpillars' appetite! Choose the planting site wisely – very hard to transplant an established plant because of its long tap root.

Planting Tips: Plant in spring or fall in average to sandy soil in an area with excellent drainage.

Fertilizer: A very light scattering (1/4 handful) of an all-purpose fertilizer in spring is plenty.

Pruning: Remove faded flowers to encourage new blossoms. Trim stems back in late fall, leaving 3-4" to mark where the plant is, as it is one of the last perennials to sprout in the spring.

Dividing/Sharing: Not an easy plant to divide or share as it grows from a long tap root.

Attracts: Bees, butterflies and hummingbirds.

Pests/Problems: None.

Cut Flower: Long-lasting and attractive. Mix with Black-Eyed Susans for an eye-catching arrangement.

Zones: 3-9

Additional Variety:

Hello Yellow – yellow gold, 20" x 2'

Gardener's Notes:

_____

_____

_____

_____

_____

_____

> *I perhaps owe having become a painter to flowers.*
> *– Claude Monet*

Cheddar Pinks

Full sun
Soft pink to magenta blooms
Blue-grey-green foliage
4-12"t and spreading
Evergreen

Cheddar Pinks are heat-tolerant mounds or mats of blue-gray to gray-green needle-like foliage lasting all year long, growing 3-12" tall. All the varieties add a nice calming color to the summer garden and some much-needed color in the winter (in warm climates).

Blossom: Very fragrant blooms ranging from soft pink to magenta are produced on erect 9-12" stems. The fringed petals look as if they were cut with pinking shears, therefore the name "pinks."

Foliage: Depending on the variety, the gray to green foliage offers different looks – Bath's Pink produces a low carpet whereas Firewitch has a mounded look.

Light: Full sun in well-drained soil.

Water: Regular watering, but does not like wet feet. Do not use mulch around the base, as this can cause fungal diseases. Gravel can be used instead.

Use: Looks especially nice in a rock garden, as an edging along a sidewalk or a patio, and as a groundcover. Bath's Pink is great draping over a wall. Firewitch does very well in containers year round.

Planting Tips: Needs to be planted in well-drained, medium-fertile soil – a sloped area is perfect. If drainage will be a problem, place the plant so the base is above the soil level by 1" or so.

Fertilizer: A light application of a time-released fertilizer or 10-10-10 scattered every spring is enough.

44

Pruning: Deadhead after each blooming period by shearing off the spent blossoms including the stems down to the foliage – using scissors works well. This will encourage more blooms throughout the season and maintain a neat appearance.

Dividing/Sharing: To keep the plants healthy, divide every 2-3 years in the spring, especially if the Bath's Pink variety starts to open up in the center.

Attracts: Butterflies.

Pests/Problems: Root rot can be a problem because of poor drainage.

Cut Flower: Very nice for a small bouquet – it has a great fragrance.

Zones: 3-9

Favorite Varieties:

    Bath's Pink – pink, 3-12" mat-forming
    Firewitch – magenta, 3-10" mound
    Plumaris – white, 3-12"
    Tiny Rubies – ruby-red, 3" low mat

Gardener's Notes:

Coreopsis – Threadleaf

Full sun
Small, daisy-like blooms
Thin, airy green foliage
1-2't x 2'w
Deciduous

Threadleaf Coreopsis is one of the toughest perennials you can grow, regarded as an Old Faithful among gardeners. The feathery foliage has a very soft, mounding appearance and is covered with dozens of daisy-like blooms from late spring into early fall.

Blossom: Small blooms are at the tips of the stems all summer long, often into fall. Shades of yellow are the most common, with many new color varieties on the market.

Foliage: Medium green, fine needle-like leaves on sturdy stems, adding an airy, loose look to the garden.

Light: Full sun, will droop if in too much shade.

Water: Very tolerant of drought and neglect, once it settles in. Coreopsis is not very happy when the soil stays continuously moist.

Use: Looks nice set against plants with larger, darker leaves. Plant in groups of three or more for a bigger show of the small blooms in the front of a garden or by a mailbox. Perfect to hide bare legs of other plants. Also good in a container, as the foliage stays attractive for so long.

Planting Tips: Does not need too much in the way of soil amendments, another reason it is such a popular plant!

Fertilizer: Add compost or a light application of fertilizer over the area every spring. Too much fertilizer will cause floppy plants.

Plant Support: None needed if growing in full sun.

Pruning: Not necessary to remove spent blooms for more flowers, but it does help. Use shears to cut plant off by one-third after first blooming period – it's too tedious to cut the stems off individually. Cut back to ground in the late fall.

Dividing/Sharing: Dig up entire clump every three years and separate with a shovel or garden knife. Replant in a new spot or share!

Attracts: Bees, butterflies and birds.

Pests/Problems: Prone to root rot in heavy wet soils. Not browsed by deer.

Cut Flower: Long lasting, a nice addition to a small bouquet.

Zones: 5-9

Varieties:

    Moonbeam – pale yellow blooms, 1-2' tall
    Zagreb – golden yellow blooms, 1-1.5' tall
    Route 66 – red/yellow blooms, 1-1.5' tall

Gardener's Notes:

TIP
Weeds need to be pulled to prevent their seed heads from producing even more weeds!

Coreopsis – Tickseed

Full sun
Yellow bloom
Medium green foliage
6"-2't x 1'w, spreading
Deciduous

Tickseed Coreopsis is a mainstay in the front portion of my garden for a few good reasons. It is easily grown, does not need perfect soil, and the foliage stays nice and compact all season long with vibrant yellow blooms welcoming the early summer season.

Blossom: The 1-2" round daisy-like yellow blooms appear at the top of a leafless 12-15" single stem. Springtime is when Tickseed blooms the heaviest, but it will continue on and off throughout the season, especially if deadheaded.

Foliage: The spoon-shaped leaves, said to resemble mouse ears, are medium green, about 2-4" long. The foliage forms a small mound that does spread but is not invasive. Useful as a ground cover for small areas.

Light: Full sun, afternoon shade is appreciated in the heat of the summer.

Water: Regular watering is best, but can withstand temporary drought conditions. Will not last long in heavy, wet soil.

Use: Plant in the front of the garden as low-growing foliage. Works well as an edging plant even once the blooms are done. Good companions are Asters (short varieties), Lamb's Ear, Upright Sedums. Looks good in containers mixed with other sun lovers, especially annuals.

Planting Tips: Plant in average, loose, well-drained soil. If the soil is too rich with compost, the plants tend to slump over.

Fertilizer: Light application (1/4 handful) each spring when new growth appears or a fresh layer of compost/mulch.

Plant Support: Not necessary.

Pruning: As blooms fade, trim off with shears at the base individually (time consuming!) or wait until the first flush of blooms is done and seed pods appear, then cut entire plant back to foliage. This will neaten up the plant, and more blooms may surprise you.

Dividing/Sharing: In late fall or early spring, dig up entire plant and divide the roots with a shovel or a garden knife. Doing this every 2-3 years will keep the plant healthy.

Attracts: Butterflies and birds love the seed pods.

Pests/Problems: Not bothered by deer. If aphids appear, use an insecticidal soap spray.

Cut Flower: Nice in a bouquet, just be sure to cut enough stems to make an impact because the single bloom on a stem is very dainty.

Zones: 4-9

Popular Varieties:

Nana – golden bloom, 6-12', compact variety
C. grandiflora/lanceolata (often listed as similar)
Sunray – double golden-yellow blooms, 2' tall
Brown eyes – yellow daisies with brown splotches, 2' tall
Early Sunrise – deep yellow, compact, 1.5' tall

Gardener's Notes:

_____

_____

_____

_____

_____

_____

_____

Crocosmia

Full sun
Trumpet-shaped blooms
Long, thin leaves
2-3' clumps
Deciduous

Crocosmia is a sturdy, tall plant that adds eye-catching colors and vertical textures to the back of the perennial garden. It does spread, so allow plenty of room!

Blossom: Varieties include hot colors – orange, red, and yellow. The small trumpet-shaped blooms are very showy, almost regal, hanging gracefully along the arching stems. Flowers appear in mid to late summer.

Foliage: Arching clumps of thin, sword-shaped leaves, similar to that of daylilies. Within a couple of years, they will grow into a 3'x3' clump.

Light: Full sun to part shade.

Water: Regular watering is best to stand tall, but can tolerate some temporary drought. The roots will rot in consistently wet soils.

Use: Perfect in front of a wall or fence, behind low shrubs or anywhere an airy splash of color is needed. A mass planting, mixed with other hot colors or with deep purple for contrast, does the job for naturalizing a slope. Good in large containers for a tall, loose look, but needs to be divided every couple years.

Planting Tips: The roots (corms) need to be planted 2" deep, 3" apart in well-drained, enriched soil. Mulch around the roots.

Fertilizer: Not much is needed, but a time-released fertilizer in the spring or a fresh layer of compost is always beneficial.

Plant Support: Use single-ring stakes or a bamboo stake/tie for stems that lean over too much once in full bloom. Another solution is to plant near sturdy, shorter shrubs for support.

Pruning: Foliage and spent blooms (berries) can be left to keep the texture in your garden until frost. Trim off all foliage to the ground at end of season.

Dividing/Sharing: In late fall or early spring, as the plant emerges from the ground, divide by digging up entire plant and splitting with a shovel, or simply dig or pull some of the plant away from main clump to replant.

Attracts: Butterflies and hummingbirds.

Pests/Problems: Thrips and spider mites, if plants become stressed. Spray with an insecticidal soap. Deer resistant.

Cut Flower: Great as a cut flower – long lasting and the leaves add a nice texture to a floral arrangement. The spent blooms (berries) are attractive in a fall bouquet.

Zones: 5-9

Crocosmia hybrids:

Lucifer – scarlet-red
Citronella – light yellow with dark eye
Spitfire – orange-red

Gardener's Notes:

_____

_____

_____

_____

TIP
Place a rock in deep bird baths
for the smaller birds to rest on.

Fairy Rose

Full sun
Light rosy pink rosettes
Small bright green leaves
2-3't x 3-5'w
Deciduous

The Fairy Rose is not normally listed as a perennial, but it is one of the best flowering plants in my garden. A sweet, but very tough small rose bush that blooms continually, even with neglect! The low-spreading shape is ideal planted among shrubs and perennials.

Blooms: Starting in late-spring and continuing until a hard freeze, dark pink small buds open to rosy pink, ruffled rosettes 1-1.5" in diameter forming large clusters along arching stems. Slight fragrance.

Foliage: Small and shiny, bright green leaves appear in March on thorny branches. Can be trained as a standard (tree form).

Light: Full sun, fine with some afternoon shade.

Water: Once established after a season or two, it is drought resistant. Until then, water deeply during times of drought.

Use: Plant against a dark green background for an outstanding contrast. Use as a specimen shrub, mixed in with perennials, planted as a low hedge or in a large container. The arching stems full of blooms make it a great choice to plant atop a low wall or on a slope, to really show it off.

Planting Tips: Amend the planting area with compost to have very loose and fertile soil. The hole should be wide enough to spread the roots out. The depth should be the same as the plant was in its container, with the base of the stem a bit higher than lower in the ground.

Fertilizer: Top dress in the spring with cow manure, and add mulch to keep the roots cool. Use either chemical or organic rose fertilizer throughout the season, following the label directions.

Plant Support: When the clusters of flowers become heavy and begin to droop, use a single-ring support or stakes/twine for support.

Pruning: During the growing season, trim off old bloom clusters as they fade to promote more blooming and keep a tidy appearance. In late fall/early spring, trim back to about 1-2', shaping up the entire plant. Blooms on new wood.

Dividing/Sharing: Cannot be divided by the roots. Use the grafting or cuttings method as with any rose bush.

Attracts: Hummingbirds and bees.

Pests/Problems: Very resistant to black spot, mildew and rust – the normal rose bush problems. Use an insecticidal soap if any insects do appear.

Cut Flower: Cut a stem full of clusters before they are fully open. They look wonderful in a vase by themselves or mixed with perennials and various foliage plants such as Sweetbox, Hostas, and Coleus.

Zones: 4-9

Gardener's Notes:

_____

_____

_____

_____

Ghost Fern

Full to part shade
No blooms
Silvery grey fronds
2't x 2-3'w
Deciduous

Ghost Fern is one of my new favorite plants in the garden. It has luminous fronds that seem to glow in the landscape. It is a very versatile fern that tolerates drought better than other Athyrium Ferns.

Foliage: The tall, rigidly-upright fronds have a silvery grey cast, turning a darker shade later in the season.

Light: Part to full shade, however, I have one in quite a bit of morning sun, and it is very content.

Water: Regular watering is best, but it can handle temporary drought.

Use: Looks great as a single specimen near a boulder, a bench, a gate, or among other ferns and shade-loving plants. Used in a mass planting, the neat and tidy vertical fronds form a delightful backdrop – the area will seem to glow with the interesting color. The bright foliage of Hostas or Heucheras placed at its feet will really set it off. Perfect as the tall element in summer shade containers.

Planting Tips: Loosen soil deeply, add compost and plant shallowly in a well-drained area, as it does not tolerate wet feet. When planting in a group, space about 1' apart. Does not do well in areas with tree root competition as it will dry out and the fronds will turn brown.

Fertilizer: A layer of manure or compost over the planting area will reward you with a healthy, vigorous fern.

Pruning: Trim off tattered fronds at the base as needed. Leave the dead foliage on after frost until the new tender fronds emerge in the spring to help protect the roots – that is, if you can take the messy look!

Dividing/Sharing: Dig up entire plant, slice the root ball in sections with a shovel or knife to replant in more areas or to share.

Pests/Problems: Root rot from too much moisture.

Zones: 9-1

Gardener's Notes:

_____

_____

_____

_____

Goldenrod

Full sun
Plumes of yellow flowers
Medium green low foliage
18-48"t x 2-3'w
Deciduous

Solidago is not the weedy roadside plant that is blamed for hay fever – that is Ragweed! However, it does have the same tough spirit, blooming in late summer to early fall, adding a striking golden color and fluffy texture to the fall garden.

Blossom: Golden-yellow clusters of tiny flowers forming a plume-like panicle or spike in the fall.

Foliage: Lance-shaped or oval, toothed, sometimes hairy on a stiff stem.

Light: Full sun to part shade.

Water: Prefers moist, well-drained soil. Then again, most varieties can take some drought and still bloom nicely.

Use: Combine with other drought-tolerant perennials such as Coneflower, Black-Eyed Susan, Asters and Ornamental Grasses for an informal look. Just the plant for a naturalized meadow setting.

Planting Tips: Solidago prefers soil that is not too fertile – this will cause the plant to grow quickly, spread and flop over instead of standing erect. But do add some amendments if the soil is hard clay or dry as a bone.

Fertilizer: A fresh layer of compost in the spring should be sufficient – too many nutrients will cause leggy plants.

Plant Support: Use short single-ring supports if the blooms become too heavy for the stem.

Pruning: Trim back in the spring by about one-third and then to the ground in the late fall.

Dividing/Sharing: In the spring or fall, dig up entire clump and separate. Best divided every two-three years to ensure healthy and vigorous plants.

Attracts: Butterflies and bees.

Pests: None.

Cut Flower: A nice addition to fall arrangements. Best to cut before the blooms are fully open.

Zones: 3/4-10

Top Varieties:

Golden Fleece – 24" mat-forming foliage
Cloth of Gold – 18"
Crown of Rays – 2-3'
Fireworks – 3-4'

Gardener's Notes:

_____

_____

_____

_____

Green & Gold

Part shade
Small, yellow blooms
Bright green leaves
6-8"t and spreads
Semi-evergreen

Chrysogonum has green leaves and gold blossoms, just as the name implies. It is a mat-forming, tough plant that works well as a ground cover but is not invasive. It is one of the first plants to bloom in the spring, with a pretty welcoming yellow blossom. One of my favorites for many years!

Blossom: Small, bright yellow 1.5" daisy-like blooms grow on a 6-8" stem. Blooms heavily in early spring and continues sporadically into the fall.

Foliage: Medium green heart-shaped leaves, about 3-4" tall.

Light: Part shade (morning sun) is best. Can tolerate more sun as long as it is planted in consistently moist soil.

Water: Thrives with regular watering, but does survive temporary dry conditions.

Use: Looks great scattered among rocks, as an edging plant in the front of a garden or as a groundcover in small areas.

Planting Tips: The soil should be amended to be very loose and fertile for the roots to take hold and send the runners to multiply.

Fertilizer: 10-10-10 or time-released fertilizer is fine for this plant in March and again lightly in May. Covering the root areas with compost is very beneficial.

Plant Support: Not necessary.

Pruning: Trim off old blooms and stems when they are finished blooming, as that may stimulate even more of the pretty yellow blossoms.

Dividing/Sharing: An easy chore – with a trowel or shovel, dig up the plants, separate the roots by hand or just remove a section away from the mother plant to replant in a new area or to share.

Pests/Problems: Mildew may appear on the foliage if very high humidity is present for an extended period. Remove infected foliage if unsightly.

Cut Flower: No

Zones: 5-8

Gardener's Notes:

_____

_____

_____

_____

Green & Gold – Part Shade

Heuchera – Coral Bells

Partial shade
Tiny white-pink blooms
Variety of foliage colors
12–24"t x 12-18"w
Evergreen

Heucheras are one of the best evergreen foliage plants for a part-shade area. There are so many colorful varieties to choose from to brighten up any garden throughout the growing season. This is a very tough and long-lasting favorite of mine, adding mounds of gorgeous foliage colors and textures to the garden as well as in containers year round.

Bloom: Tiny bell-shaped blooms appear on thin, 2-3' tall, wiry stems from late spring to fall, creating a pretty, airy look. However, many gardeners remove these stems to keep the foliage the star of the show.

Foliage: The 3-5" leaves are round, heart-shaped or triangular. They can be smooth, wavy or ruffled on a sturdy but flexible stem. Colors range from burgundy to chartreuse to peachy orange, with the underside a complementary shade. Gorgeous!!

Light: Overall, most varieties do best in morning sun and afternoon shade. In the winter, they will tolerate almost full-day sun in the southern zones.

Water: Performs best in evenly moist conditions. That said, Heucheras tend to be drought tolerant.

Use: Heucheras are wonderful as a single plant placed among ferns, hostas, impatiens or with pansies in the winter garden. Attractive snuggled up against boulders. A mass of plants is great as a groundcover. Combining two or three different Heucheras, such as Citronelle and Pinot Noir, is a unique way to add color to your gardens using foliage instead of blossoms.

Planting Tips: The soil needs to be amended with a good amount of compost. Because Heucheras have shallow roots, plant the crowns (roots) about 1" below the soil surface to keep them from drying out too quickly. They can tolerate varied growing environments – experiment with different varieties and placements!

Fertilizer: Adding composted leaves and mulch around the plant base each spring will add nutrients as well as keep the crowns cool.

Plant Support: Not necessary.

Pruning: In early spring, remove all tattered foliage and stems at the base. Throughout the season, trim off any foliage that is sun scorched or broken off.

Dividing/Sharing: After a few seasons, Heucheras tend to heave up out of the ground – remove a few sections, toss away any dead portions and replant with plenty of compost. Share the extra plants or use in afternoon shade containers, where they look great.

Attracts: Butterflies and hummingbirds.

Pests/Problems: Deer resistant. Mealy bugs may appear near the base and can be controlled with an insecticidal soap. Leaf scorch may happen if planted in hot, full sun. Overly wet winter conditions can cause root rot.

Cut Flower: Cut the flower stems when the buds are just opening. Use the foliage to add interesting color and texture to arrangements – very long lasting!

Zones: 4-9

A Few Favorite Varieties (all are tolerant of heat and humidity):

Beaujolais: burgundy leaves with a touch of silvering and deeper purple veins. A vigorous and large variety.

Caramel: new leaves emerge a glowing caramel and mature to a soft peachy-orange and maroon underside, adding warmth and contrast. Can take a good amount of sun.

Citronelle: solid lime-yellow leaves, complementing dark-foliaged plants, especially blues and purples. Creamy white blooms in the summer. Morning sun is best.

(continued)

(Heuchera – Coral Bells, continued)

Mocha: coffee-colored foliage darkens in the sun. A mounded, compact plant with pleasant layering.

Pinot Noir: dark purple leaves in spring become more purple as the season progresses with a silvery overlay and dark purple veining. Produces white flowers in mid-summer.

Tiramisu: chartreuse foliage with touches of brick red in both the spring and fall. During the summer, the leaves lighten to chartreuse with a light silvery cast.

Gardener's Notes:

_____

_____

_____

_____

_____

_____

_____

_____

_____

_____

Heuchera, Hosta, Astilbe – Part shade

Holly Fern

Part to full shade
No blooms
Dark green foliage
18-30"t x 24-36"w
Evergreen

The Holly Fern resembles a small shrub more than a fern when full grown. It is an upright, vase-shaped plant with spiny-edged leaves on arching stems. Only those gardeners living in zones 7-10 will be the lucky ones to grow this beautiful fern year after year.

Foliage: Glossy dark green, with bright green new growth, 2-3" long pointed leaves on arching sturdy stems.

Light: Morning sun is fine, but needs afternoon shade or all-day light shade.

Water: Ample moisture is best in the first couple of seasons for this fern to become fully established. During times of drought, be sure to give it a weekly watering, especially if it is in two or more hours of direct sun.

Use: Attractive as a small hedge under windows, along a low deck, in a woodland garden or as an accent plant tucked in among other part-shade lovers, such as Astilbe, Hostas and other types of Ferns.

Planting Tips: After digging a wide hole, mix the removed soil with compost and use to fill in around the plant, making sure not to plant too deep. When planting in a grouping, place the ferns at least 2' apart – they will fill out in a couple seasons.

Fertilizer: Add Holly Tone or a similar fertilizer over the ground each spring, along with a fresh layer of manure/compost.

Plant Support: None needed.

Pruning: Late winter/early spring is the time to trim off all brown fronds damaged by the winter weather or old age. Use pruners to trim these off all the way to the ground, being careful not to remove the new fronds that will be uncurling. Remove any brown fronds during the season.

Dividing/Sharing: After a few years, the plant will multiply into sections, which makes it easy to divide in the spring. When the new fiddleheads appear, remove old fronds, dig up the whole plant, separate the sections and transplant or share with a fellow gardener.

Pests/Problems: Protect from strong winds and full sun.

Cut Flower: Adds a coarse but very attractive element to an arrangement. Long lasting.

Zones: 7-10

Varieties:

Rochfordianum – very coarsely-fringed fronds

Gardener's Notes:

_____

_____

_____

_____

TIP

When planting containers, place a coffee filter over the drainage hole in the bottom to keep soil from washing out.

Holly Fern – Variegated

Part to full shade
No blooms
Green with yellow veins
18-24"t x 18"w
Evergreen to Zone 6-7

Variegated Holly Fern has been in my yard for years and always draws the attention of visitors. It is the most strikingly colored of all ferns with a yellow band down the center of dark green fronds. In the southern states, it tolerates heat and humidity plus provides winter interest in shady areas. A slow grower, but more than worth the wait!

Foliage: The leathery-textured fronds are a dark glossy green with a center yellow band. The triangular-shaped fronds, 8" at the widest part, grow 18-24" tall on sturdy, erect stems.

Light: Shade to partial shade, morning sun is fine.

Water: For ultimate growth, regular watering is best. Nonetheless, it can withstand dry conditions.

Use: Wonderful as the accent plant, in groupings of three or more set among other ferns, especially Autumn Fern, as they share the same growing needs. Because of its open nature, it is fun to underplant with Heucheras, Hostas or Toad Lilies along with shade annuals such as Impatiens and Fancy Begonias. Pretty hugging the base of a birdbath as well as planted in a container with other shade lovers.

Planting Tips: Try to purchase the largest size available to get it off to a good start. Loosened and moist acidic soil would be the ultimate spot for this fern, but it will tolerate less than perfect conditions. If it dies back, use a plant marker to designate the fern's position, as it is late to emerge in the spring. Cover the area with a layer of mulch.

Fertilizer: Composted materials added to the hole at planting time will be the best fertilizer. Top dressing with compost each spring renews the necessary nutrients.

Plant Support: A single-ring stake works well for the tallest stems.

Pruning: Remove all browned and dried up fronds to the ground in early spring as well as during the growing season. Be careful not to cut the emerging stems!

Dividing/Sharing: Necessary to wait a couple years to divide until new plants emerge alongside the original fern.

Pests/Problems: None.

Cut Foliage: Very striking in any type of arrangement.

Zones: Evergreen in winter to Zone 6, about 10-15 degrees.

Gardener's Notes:

_____

_____

_____

_____

Hosta

Part shade/dappled shade
White/lavender bloom
All shades and sizes of leaves
6-36"t x 6-48+"w
Deciduous

Hostas are long-lived perennials that have spectacular foliage with the bloom almost being an afterthought. Most large varieties take a few years to reach their full size. Autumn produces very attractive yellow fall foliage. There are too many varieties to list, so I will describe just a few of my favorites.

Light: Part shade to dappled shade. A few hours of morning sun works well for most Hostas, depending on the moisture. Usually with more sun, the plant will be more compact.

Water: Larger leaf varieties seem to be more drought tolerant. When Hosta leaves dry out, the leaf edges will turn brown. Keeping the soil evenly moist will reward you with a happy, healthy Hosta!

Use: Hostas lend so much color and texture to the garden – small plants are perfect tucked in around rocks, medium varieties look nice grouped together as a ground cover and the large ones as an eye-catching specimen. They are also a good plant for containers as long as they are not planted too deeply.

Planting Tips: Soil should be very organic and rich with amendments for plants to do their best. Mulch should be used under the foliage to keep mud from splattering on the leaves. (Don't pile mulch up against the stem, especially if Voles are present.)

Fertilizer: A time-released fertilizer works well every spring along with a layer of compost. From mid to late summer, a liquid fertilizer every few weeks will keep the Hosta going strong into the fall season.

Plant Support: None is necessary.

Pruning: Trim off any damaged leaves at the base during the growing season. After the foliage turns color and then dries up in the fall, trim off at the base and discard.

Dividing/Sharing: Divide every few years to rejuvenate the plant. The plant may outgrow its space, the soil may need amending, or you may just want to move a section of a favorite Hosta to another spot or share with a friend. Best to do this chore in the spring as leaves are just poking up out of the ground. Dig up the whole plant and cut into sections with a serrated knife. Replant in amended soil.

Pests/Problems:

Slugs! Present during moist summers, they love to chew on the leaves. Heavily textured or waxy leafed Hostas are the most slug resistant. Use slug bait for best results. The beer-in-a-dish method seems to attract the alcoholic slugs in numbers!

Deer – use Deer Off or a motion sprinkler.

Voles – get a cat!

Despite the occasional pest problem, Hostas are more than worth the effort.

Cut Flower: Both the leaves and the flower stalks are great to use in arrangements.

Zones: 3-10, depending on the variety.

A Few Favorite Varieties:

August Moon: Oval-shaped, lightly-crinkled, bright chartreuse leaves. White flowers. 1.5't x 2.5'w

Frances Williams: Heart-shaped, puckered grey-green leaves with yellowish-green edges. Early pale lavender blooms. 2-3't x 3'w

Honeybells: Wavy-edged light green leaves. Nicely scented, late summer pale lilac blooms. 2-3't x 4'w

June: Beautiful blue-green edges with a chartreuse center of the leaf. Lavender blooms in mid-season. 1.5-2't x 1.5'w

(continued)

(Hosta – continued)

Krossa Regal: Leathery, silver-blue large leaves make a vase-shaped clump. Late bloomer with 5-6' tall lavender flower spikes. Slug resistant. 3't x 3'w

Patriot: Heart-shaped green leaves with a wide, white edge. Lavender blooms. 1.5't x 3'w

Sum & Substance: Large, textured chartreuse leaves with lavender flowers. Slug resistant. Fairly sun tolerant. 3't x 5'w

Gardener's Notes:

_____

_____

_____

_____

TIP
Beat the summer sun:

Use sunscreen

Wear UV clothing

Wear a hat – top of head is very susceptible to sun

Wear a sweatband – keeps the sweat from dripping into your eyes!

Toad Lily, Bleeding Heart, Lenten Rose, Ferns – Shade

Iris

Full sun to light shade
Vast array of colors
Sword-shaped leaves
6"-4't x 1-2+'w
Deciduous

The Bearded Iris has always been one of the most popular perennials due to its longevity as well as the beauty of the blossom in the spring/summer garden. Easy to grow, it will reward you with gorgeous blossoms as well as a different shape and texture with the foliage.

Blossom: Each blossom has six petals, three of which point up or out and three of which point down or out. The "bearded" reference is the band of hairs on the drooping petals. All colors and combinations of the rainbow (except true red and green) make it difficult to choose just a few varieties for the average-sized garden! Late spring to early summer blooming period.

Foliage: Sword-shaped leaves have a bluish cast. They are about 2" wide and 6"-4' tall, depending on the variety.

Light: Full sun. Less blooms in more shade.

Water: Needs plenty of water for a few weeks after planting for the roots to take hold. Make sure the soil drains well – does not survive in wet soil as this causes rot. Very drought tolerant after the first season.

Use: In the perennial garden, a single Iris, a grouping of one color, or a mixture of colors can't be beat. A perfect plant in containers, by a mailbox or gate, anywhere you need a tall, spiky texture.

Planting Tips: To achieve a full look, plant at least three plants together. Add compost/soil conditioner to produce loose soil about 6-12" deep. Place each rhizome (roots/tubers) with the ends/tips toward each other to form a triangle, 6" apart so that the tops of the rhizome are just above the soil surface, after it has been watered in. Best to plant in early fall.

Fertilizer: Use a bulb fertilizer (approximately 6-12-12) to mix with the soil when planting. Each spring, toss a small handful over the emerging foliage and again after blooming has finished.

Plant support: Single-loop stakes work well for the stems once they are loaded with blooms.

Pruning: Remove any diseased/brown leaves during the season to prevent the spread of disease. When the blooms have faded, trim the flower stems off at the base. In the fall before frost, cut all the foliage off at ground level.

Dividing/Sharing: August to September is the best time to divide Irises, every 3-4 years. Dig up the entire clump and remove any rotten/diseased rhizome and replant in amended soil. Water well for a few weeks. Always a good plant to pass along to fellow gardeners.

Pests: Iris borers are worm-like larvae that attack and hollow out the rhizome. To prevent them, pull off and destroy any old brown leaves as the borer lays eggs in the leaves. Try to keep all debris off the top of the rhizomes. To control occasional aphids on the leaves, spray off with the hose or use the Ivory Soap spray. Deer resistant.

Cut Flower: Yes – doesn't last very long, but worth it! When the flowers begin to open, cut the stem above the white part of the stem. Dip the stem in boiling water for one minute, then into deep cool water.

Zones: 3-10

Varieties: Local nurseries along with garden catalogs will have a list of locally-available plants.

Gardener's Notes:

_____

_____

_____

_____

Japanese Painted Fern

Part to full shade
No blooms
Silvery-white fronds
1-2't x 18-30"w
Deciduous

Japanese Painted Fern is the brightest fern for the shady garden, adding strong contrast against greens and burgundy plants, while being one of the easiest ferns to grow.

Foliage: The slowly spreading clumps are formed with weeping fronds that have wine-red stems and fronds with green centers and silvery-white tips.

Light: Part shade to full shade. Morning sun is fine with adequate moisture.

Water: Keep soil evenly moist, and water deeply during times of drought, as it will wither. However, it does reappear the next season after a temporary drought.

Use: Many areas in the garden will benefit from this light-colored fern – it is beautiful in the front to middle areas set against dark green plants such as Cast-Iron Plant, blue-toned Hostas, burgundy Heucheras, tucked in between mossy or grey rocks and pretty with the height of Solomon's Seal. As with most ferns, it does have somewhat brittle fronds, so do not plant it in areas highly traveled by children or dogs!

Planting Tips: Dig a good-sized hole and add lots of compost. Water every other day for a week to ensure a good start.

Fertilizer: Compost added at planting time and each spring over the roots will suffice.

Pruning: Trim off any fronds during the season that turn brown from drought or are broken. In late fall, remove fronds after frost – or they can be left for insulation during the winter if that look is ok for you.

Dividing/Sharing: Transplanting is easy with this fern since the root ball is not very large. A mature plant will have many offspring around the base. As you dig these up, make sure there are roots attached to each new plant.

Pests: None that I have noticed.

Cut Foliage: Doesn't work well as the fronds dry out too quickly.

Zones: 3-8

Additional varieties:
Silver Falls
Ursula's Red – more red than 'Pictum'

Gardener's Notes:

_____

_____

_____

_____

Kind hearts are the gardens, kind thoughts are the roots.

Kind words are the flowers, kind hearts are the fruits.

Take care of your garden and keep out the weeds,

Fill it with sunshine, kind words and kind deeds.

– Longfellow 1807-1882

Knock Out Rose

Full sun
Red, pink or yellow blossom
Green foliage
3-5't x 3-4'w
Deciduous

The Knock Out Rose has become a very popular low-maintenance plant with good reason. Compared to traditional rose varieties, it requires little care: drought tolerant, disease resistant, mildew tolerant, produces numerous blooms per branch throughout the season and is self-cleaning. What more can I say?! My favorite color is the Red Knock Out – the cherry red – it is so vibrant in the garden!

Blossom: Colors available are red, yellow and pink – single as well as double forms. The blooming starts in spring and continues on and off until frost.

Foliage: Dark green with a purple tint that turns burgundy in late fall.

Light: Full sun, can take a few hours of light shade in the afternoon.

Water: Moderate water, but able to withstand some drought. When hand-watering, direct the water on the soil around the rose, not the foliage, to prevent leaf spot problems.

Use: Attractive as a specimen for a pop of color, en masse in a single color or mixed colors, in a grouping in front of an evergreen background or wall, in the back of a mixed border. Wherever it is planted, give it plenty of room to spread out and grow.

Planting Tips: Choose a spot 4-5' from another plant or structure as well as from each other (on center). Dig the hole 6" deeper and wider than the root ball. Mix in compost and rose fertilizer. Mulch around plants.

Fertilizer: Use a fertilizer developed for roses, following directions on the label.

Pruning: In early spring remove the old brown canes (stems) to the ground. Next, trim the green canes to one-half the desired height when the rose is in bloom i.e., for a height of 3', trim to 1.5'.

During the long blooming period, prune to keep a nice shape – remove any branches that are growing faster than others and cut off spent flowers to let the new blooms show through. Compared to traditional roses, it is self-cleaning.

Don't worry; there isn't an incorrect pruning method to harm this rose!

Dividing/Sharing: Cannot be divided by the shovel method. Rose propagation methods work best.

Pests/Problems: In normal conditions, disease and pest free. A systemic product or insecticidal soap is helpful if any pests appear.

Cut Flower: Roses are always a great addition to any arrangement. Choose blooms that are not fully open for a longer-lasting display.

Zones: 4-11

Available Color Varieties:
Red
Pink
Sunny – yellow to cream
Blushing – light pink

Gardener's Notes:

_____

_____

_____

_____

_____

_____

Lady Fern

Part to full shade
No blooms
Green, feathery fronds
1-3't x 1-3'w
Deciduous

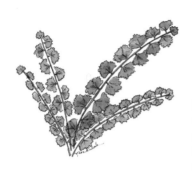

Lady Fern is perfect for the novice as well as seasoned gardener. Many fancy cultivated types are available along with the traditional upright clumping variety, all with a very delicate and fine appearance, but very hardy. They may need some extra care the first year or two but take off with added moisture, compost and patience.

Foliage: From light and airy upright fronds with a light yellow-green color, to varieties having low-growing fronds with little balls of leaves along the stems. All add different shades of green and texture to the shade garden or container.

Light: Does best in partial to full shade – but, with plenty of moisture, more sun is tolerated. Just not the afternoon summer sun – it will scorch the foliage.

Water: Evenly moist soil will reward you with full, lush plants. When hand-watering, try to water only the soil around the roots, as using a hard spray on the fronds will break them.

Use: A wonderful addition to the shade garden planted among other species of ferns as well as Hostas, Hardy Begonias, and Impatiens. Perfect to use for mass plantings along a streambed, near a gate or a shaded mailbox area. Because of their highly brittle fronds, as with most ferns, do not use in high traffic or windy areas.

Planting Tips: Before planting, work the soil deeply, adding rotted leaves or compost to mimic the native woodland soil. Do not plant too deeply, keeping the crown at the soil level. Use mulch year round.

Fertilizer: Spreading a layer of manure or composted leaves around the roots each spring is all that is needed.

Plant Support: Not necessary unless wind or rain has caused them to collapse.

Pruning: Trim off at the base any broken or tattered fronds during the season to promote new growth. It's a personal choice whether to trim off brown fronds after frost or wait until spring clean-up time.

Dividing/Sharing: To keep the plants vigorous, dig up the whole plant every few years, divide with a shovel and replant. Spring is the best time to divide clumps for sharing or adding more to your yard – with the new growth visible, it's easier to remember where there are planted!

Pests/Problems: Dogs and children!

Cut Flower: Try the different varieties for unique additions to any arrangement.

Zones: 3-8

Favorite Varieties:

Lady Fern (upright) – bright green, 2't x 2+'w
Cristatum (Crested) – ends of the fronds are forked or crested, 2.5't x 2'w
Frizelliae (Tatting Fern) – little half-moon balls alternating along the stems, 1't x 1.5'w

Gardener's Notes:

_____

_____

_____

_____

_____

_____

Lamb's Ear

Full sun to light shade
Light grey foliage
1.5't X 2'w
Evergreen

The 'Countess Helene von Stein' aka Big Ears, is the best of the Lamb's Ears for most of us in the country to plant. It is the most tolerant of heat and humidity. The soft, gray foliage is the star of the show – so attractive in the garden, creating a pleasant edging for any garden bed.

Foliage: The 6-10" tongue-shaped leaves are soft and thick, with a light grey, almost white, coloring. They have a wonderful, soft feel – like a Lamb's Ear!

Light: Likes full sun, but does fine with some relief from the afternoon sun.

Water: Moderate moisture, can survive dry periods. Does not hold up well in constant summer rains.

Use: Plant in the front of the garden against dark colors to really show it off. Mixes well with summer pastels. Perfect as an edging along a walkway, in the mailbox area, as a ground cover, most anywhere to add a pleasant contrast in color and texture – try it in a container.

Planting Tips: Not too fussy about the soil, can even take sandy soil. Needs good drainage, or plant crowns may rot.

Fertilizer: A light application of an organic fertilizer in the spring is sufficient.

Pruning: Trim or pull off old leaves that get mushy with too much rain and heat; this will keep the plant looking fresh. Cut back the stems coming from the crown when it becomes leggy. Cooler weather brings new foliage that usually stays in mild climates.

Divide/Share: Overcrowding may happen in a few years, so spring is a good time to dig up sections, divide and replant in another area in your yard or share with others. The foliage may look stressed after transplanting but reestablishes quickly.

Pests/Problems: Not bothered by deer. Poor drainage can be a major problem, as can long, rainy summers – the foliage soaks up the moisture, creating a mushy mess that is easily taken care of by removing these leaves. Will resprout quickly.

Cut Flower: The woolly leaves add a nice texture to any arrangement.

Zones: 4-7

Gardener's Notes:

_____

_____

_____

_____

Lamb's Ear, Green & Gold – Part sun

Lenten Rose

Part shade to full shade
White to maroon blooms
Large, leathery foliage
2't x 2.5'w clumps
Evergreen

Lenten Rose is a species of Helleborous that is very easy to grow, long-lived, and looks wonderful all year long in shade gardens, so welcome in the winter months. It has large, evergreen leaves with blossoms that begin in February and last all spring.

Blossom: Cup-shaped, 2-3" blossoms face downward with a nodding effect. Colors range from white to maroon. They last for a couple months and eventually fade to a nice light green and then brown – time to clip them off.

Foliage: The leaves are shiny, dark green and leathery – very elegant looking. They resemble a large star, the clump growing approximately 12-16" wide.

Light: Partial to full shade. Too much sun causes the plant to be less vigorous.

Water: Best in a moist, woodland soil. However, as the plant ages, it becomes more drought tolerant.

Use: Looks great as a single plant, as masses to form a groundcover, along the top of a wall or on a slope so the cupped blooms are easily seen. Very pretty mixed in with other shade-lovers, such as Hostas, Ferns, Heucheras, Solomon's Seal and summer annuals – Impatiens and Begonias. Great in a container that is well drained.

Planting Tips: Plant in soil that has been loosened, rich in organic matter and well drained.

Fertilizer: Scatter an organic or a time-released product every spring, and top dress with composted material.

Pruning: Trim off old leaves to the base (usually lying on the ground or browned from winter burn) in late winter/early spring to enjoy the new growth and blooms that are emerging. Remove old blooms down to the base once they have turned brownish, usually by May.

Dividing/Sharing: Best not to divide plants, but they can be moved in early spring. After a couple years, each plant will have many seedlings at its base, which are simple to dig up and transplant or share.

Pests: None; deer can pass them by!

Cut Flower: Beautiful in arrangements, but does need some preparation. Scald the stem ends in boiling water, prick the stem along the total length with a needle and then place in deep water in a vase.

Zones: 4-9

Gardener's Notes:

_____

_____

_____

_____

TIP

Plastic grocery bags work great to store transplants in for a while – just add water to keep the roots hydrated.

Oxalis

Full sun to part shade
Pink, white or yellow blossom
Green or purple foliage
4-10"t x 1'w
Deciduous

Oxalis, also known as Shamrocks, can add a unique look and texture to any garden. Years ago, I bought a bag of the little bulbs, not sure what they were. I have so enjoyed the purple mounds popping up here and there in my gardens – I love the spark of color they add. The varieties I recommend are not the weedy member of the Oxalis family many gardeners fear!

Blossom: A 1" funnel-shaped bloom composed of five petals at the top of a slender stalk just above the foliage. Blooms on and off from May to October. The color, from white to pink to red, depends on the variety.

Foliage: The leaves fold downward at night, opening up in the morning to reveal three or more heart-shaped leaves resembling a clover plant. Colors range from purple and black, green and silver to bright purple or plain old green!

Light: Full sun to partial shade, especially in the afternoon.

Water: Grows best with consistent moisture in the summer, but can definitely survive drought conditions. Does not do well with wet feet in the winter, as the bulbs may rot.

Use: A great accent plant for the front edge of gardens, scattered among rocks, and in woodland areas. The dark colors of the foliage seem to come alive in the garden when planted near chartreuse Hostas, Heucheras and plants with white blossoms. Fun planted in the front of a container.

Planting Tips: Plant the bulbs only 1-2" deep and 3-5" apart in amended soil.

Fertilizer: A light application each spring of a time-released product, such as Osmocote, plus a new layer of compost is sufficient.

Plant Support: None is needed.

Pruning: During the season, remove any scorched or tattered foliage as well as any spent blossoms to keep the mound looking tidy.

Dividing/Sharing: Very easy to dig up a few bulbs from the main plant to share or move to a new area in the garden.

Pests/Problems: May be susceptible to rust on the foliage in hot, humid summers. Just trim back to the ground to encourage new growth when cooler temperatures arrive.

Cut Flower: In the evening, the foliage will fold downward but pops back open in the morning – very pretty!

Zones: 6/7-10

Favorite Varieties:

Oxalis alba – bright green leaves with small white star-shaped blooms.

O. regnellii 'Silverado' – olive green leaves with a bright silver center area. White flowers.

O. tetraphylla 'Iron Cross' – medium green leaves with a purple cross shape. Reddish blooms with greenish yellow throats.

O. regnellii 'Triangularis' – deep, velvety purple leaves with a wide black border. Tiny light pink flowers.

Gardener's Notes:

_____

_____

_____

_____

Phlox

Full sun
Various bloom colors
Medium green foliage
3-4't x 2'w
Deciduous

Garden Phlox is an old-fashioned, tall, summer-flowering favorite – a long-lasting attention getter. The best foliage mildew-resistant varieties for areas with hot, humid summers are David, David's Lavender, Wild Purple and Bright Eyes.

Blossom: The flower is a 3-6" dome-shaped cluster of 1" fragrant flowers. Blooms last quite a few weeks.

Foliage: The leaves are medium green, 2-5" long and slender.

Light: Full sun, but can tolerate and often appreciates some afternoon shade.

Water: Does best in moist, well-drained soil. It may wilt in the afternoon during a drought, but the plant survives long term.

Use: Looks best in the middle to back of the garden with a shorter plant in front to hide the stems when they become a bit leggy late in the summer. Using a mixture of the different varieties in a grouping is a great way to show off the colors of a summer garden.

Planting Tips: Give this plant plenty of room to spread out, as overcrowding and lack of air circulation can cause powdery mildew on the leaves. Plant in good, loose, amended soil. Mulch to keep roots cool.

Fertilizer: A time-released product scattered over new growth in spring as well as a half inch layer of compost.

Plant support: When the spring growth is about 12" tall, place either a 3' tomato cage or a grid ring over it – much easier than trying to do it when it gets taller!

Pruning: Clip off the top of each stem about 6-8" in the spring when the plant reaches approximately 2' tall (Chelsea Chop method). Remove stems at the base to thin plants to 6-8 stems per plant every year to aid in air circulation. In the summer, as blooms fade, trim the tips off, as this will encourage re-blooming from side shoots. Cut back to a few inches in the late fall.

Dividing/Sharing: Dig up complete root ball and divide with a shovel every 3-4 years. Great plant to divide for sharing or planting in another spot in your garden – it also reseeds itself!

Pests: Red spider mite – spray with insecticidal soap. Powdery mildew – use a fungicide. If these are a problem for more than one year, use a systemic product in early spring, such as Bayer Advanced, and follow label directions.

Attracts: Butterflies and hummingbirds.

Cut Flower: Cut before the blooms are fully open, and remove leaves from the stem. It does start to drop petals after a few days but is worth the messiness!

Zones: 4-8

Mildew Resistant Varieties:
Bright Eyes – pink flower with red eye
David – white
David's Lavender – lavender pink
Wild Purple – light purple

Gardener's Notes:

_____

_____

_____

_____

_____

Pink Muhly Grass

Full sun to light shade
Rosy pink plumes
Dark green foliage
3-4't x 3-4'w
Deciduous

Pink Muhly Grass is a medium-sized, warm-season ornamental grass. An excellent choice for low-maintenance gardens as well as coastal areas given that it tolerates wind and salt. Massed together, it creates a spectacular fall show.

Blossom: Very showy, puffy plumes in a rosy-red hue, about 4-6" long, on thin stalks. Blooming in late summer/early fall until frost. If preferred, leave the dried stalks and blossoms on for winter interest until spring clean-up time.

Foliage: Dark green, very slender stalks that form a 3-4' tall and wide mound.

Light: Full sun to part shade.

Water: Very drought resistant, but does respond well with an extra watering now and then, especially during the first growing season.

Use: Place the Grass in groups of three or more so the western sun can backlight the plant for a fabulous illumination of the rosy plumes! Plant in the middle to back section of the garden against a dark background of shrubs, near boulders, surrounding a bird house, or with other late season bloomers, such as Goldenrod and Asters. Provides a nice contrast to coarse textures.

Planting Tips: Best to plant in the spring when soil temperatures have warmed up. Amend the soil in the planting area with coarse sand and soil conditioner to provide good drainage. Water thoroughly for the first month, about five gallons a week.

Fertilizer: Each spring, a small handful of all-purpose fertilizer scattered over the soil is good. Just not too much; it will cause the plant to grow too tall and flop over. Mulch.

Pruning: Shear down to 4-5" in late winter or early spring before the new growth appears.

Dividing/Sharing: Dig up with a shovel and divide every three to four years to add to your collection or share.

Pests: None noticed.

Cut Flower: The plumes are very attractive in a fall arrangement.

Zones: 6-10

Additional Varieties:
  Regal Mist – deep rosy red, 3-4't
  White Cloud – white, 4't

Gardener's Notes:

_____

_____

_____

_____

TIP
Tie a brightly colored ribbon on
your favorite small tools, such as
pruners, to find them easily.

Purple Coneflower

Full sun
Rosy-purple to red bloom
Medium green foliage
3-5't x 2'w
Deciduous

Purple Coneflower (really a rosy-purple shade) is the most popular and widely grown of the Echinaceas – a must for the novice as well as the seasoned gardener. Clumps range in size from 3-5' tall and 2' wide. The blooms are on stiff stems, perfect for the Goldfinches to sit on and nibble the seeds in the center cone.

Blossom: The bloom is about 2-3" round, with drooping, rosy-purple daisy-like petals and an orange-brown center cone. The blooming starts in mid June-July and may last until October.

Foliage: Medium green, 3-8" oblong, coarse leaves.

Light: Full sun; can take some morning shade.

Water: Moderate water. The leaves may droop, but it is fairly drought tolerant once established after the first season.

Use: Plant in back of the garden or up against a picket fence, with shorter, full plants in front to cover its legginess in late summer. Looks nice with other sun-loving standards, such as Phlox, Black-Eyed Susan, Daylilies. Works well in a mixed, large container planting for the summer season.

Planting Tips: Prepare the soil well with lots of compost. Plant clumps about 2' apart. Mulch.

Fertilizer: Sprinkle a time-released product around the plant in early spring. A liquid fertilizer poured around the roots in the summer will reward you with a nice, healthy plant for the end of the season.

Plant Support: If any is necessary, use a single-hoop stake for each leaning stem as this makes it look more natural.

Pruning: During the season, remove spent blooms along with the stem down to the next leaf to encourage more blooms. However, Goldfinches will appreciate a few seed heads left on the plant. Cut the whole plant back to the ground in the fall.

Dividing/Sharing: In late fall or early spring, dig up the entire plant, divide in sections with a shovel, replant in amended soil in a new area or share with a friend.

Attracts: Butterflies. Goldfinches love to munch on the seed pods.

Pests/Problems: An unknown virus can turn a couple stems per season black. It is best to just cut them off at the ground and discard. Deer resistant.

Cut Flower: Excellent to cut for summer arrangements, very long lasting.

Zones: 3-8

Additional Varieties:

Check with your local nursuries for new selections.

Big Sky Series – a variety of colors available
Kim's Knee High – clear pink – 2' tall
Crazy White – 18-24" tall

Gardener's Notes:

_____

_____

_____

_____

_____

Sedum – Low-Growing

Full sun to part shade
Petite, starry blooms
Small, fleshy leaves
2-8"t and spreading
Evergreen to semi-evergreen

Many varieties of this great drought-tolerant, tough plant are available and range in size, shape and color of both foliage and blooms. Sedums form a low-growing mat that adds unique textures to the garden or containers year round.

Blossom: Small, starry blooms appear on and off all season, depending on the variety. Colors range from white to pink to yellow and normally darken with age.

Foliage: Fleshy leaves are evergreen, depending on the variety and the zone. Colors can be light green to blue-gray to chartreuse.

Light: Full sun to part shade. Experiment with the many available varieties in different areas of your garden!

Water: All are very drought tolerant. They do not do well in low, moist areas.

Use: Great in so many areas. Tuck in a rock wall crevice, use as a ground cover, a border or to edge a patio or walkway. However, not great for foot traffic, as the fleshy foliage crushes easily. Also, sedums work well in containers and dish gardens, adding different colors and textures – just make sure it has excellent drainage. Perfect as the trailer for containers with other low-moisture plants such as Blue Fescue Grass and Cheddar Pinks.

Planting Tips: Do not plant in heavy clay areas, as sedums need excellent drainage. Add soil conditioner or pea gravel to the planting area. Any standing water, especially in the winter, will cause root rot.

Fertilizer: A time-released product such as Osmocote or the standard 10-10-10 lightly scattered every spring will work well.

Pruning: Not much pruning is needed except to remove old blossoms from the blooming varieties.

Dividing/Sharing: Very easy to dig up portions any time of the year to move to another area, add to a container and, of course, share with a fellow gardener.

Pests/Problems: Fungus and root rot from excess moisture.

Zones: 3-8

A Few of My Favorite Varieties:

Angelina: spiral-shaped chartreuse foliage, 2-3" tall.
Space 8-12" apart.

Blue Spruce: needle-like, bluish-green foliage, 4-6" tall.
Resembles tiny evergreen shrubs. Space 8-10" apart.

Jellybean: Small, round, medium green foliage, 1-3" tall.
White blooms. Space 10-12" apart.

Weihenstephaner Gold: Small, round, medium green
foliage, 2-3" tall. Yellow star blooms. Will grow in shade,
but not many blooms. Space 8-12" apart. Forms 1' wide clumps.

Gardener's Notes:

_____

_____

_____

_____

_____

Sedum – Upright

Full sun
Pink to bronze-red blooms
Green succulent leaves
1.5-2't x 1-2'w
Deciduous

Autumn Joy is one tough plant! It is the most widely grown of the Upright Sedums, aka "You-can't-kill-it Plant!" The fleshy leaves and ever-changing blossoms make this clump-forming sedum a favorite among gardeners to use in a wide range of areas in the landscape.

Blossom: Starting in mid summer, the pink clusters of tiny flowers atop the stems darken with time and eventually turn to an attractive bronze-red in the fall.

Foliage: Multi-stemmed clump with thick, succulent, waxy leaves, rounded in shape, 1-2" long.

Light: Full sun. Will grow in part sun, less upright.

Water: Very drought tolerant.

Use: The front to middle section of a bed with other drought-tolerant plants is a good way to view Autumn Joy's attributes. Groupings of three to five plants mixed with ornamental grasses or shrubs produce pleasing results as does a specimen tucked in by a boulder. Perfect in containers with drought-resistant shrubs and annuals.

Planting Tips: Loosen the soil in the planting hole, but rich amendments are not necessary. Too fertile of a soil will cause the sedum to grow too tall, open in the center and collapse. Provide good drainage to prevent root and crown rot.

Fertilizer: A covering of the soil with compost or mulch provides enough nutrients.

Pruning: In the spring when the new growth reaches about 1', remove 4-6" from the top of the Sedum to produce a sturdier plant. Many gardeners enjoy the look of the dried blossoms left on the plant going into the winter. Or...remove all stems down to the ground before a hard freeze.

Dividing/Sharing: Needs to be divided every few years to control the size. Dig up entire clump with a shovel and divide into sections, discarding dried-up roots, and replant in a container, in new areas, or give away.

Attracts: Various butterflies and bees.

Pests/Problems: Occasional aphids can be controlled with an insecticidal soap. Too much water can be a problem, causing rot.

Cut Flower: Lasts longer if the blooms are not quite fully opened when cut from the plant.

Zones: 2-8

Additional Varieties:

Vera Jameson – Burgandy foliage, pink blossoms
Maestro – Green foliage, pink blossoms
Variegated – Green and cream foliage with pink blossoms

Gardener's Notes:

_____

_____

_____

_____

Variegated Upright Sedum

Leucanthemum x superbum

Shasta Daisy

Full sun
Medium green leaves
White daisy bloom
3't x 3'w
Deciduous

Shasta Daisies are one of my favorite summer-blooming plants – so many long-lasting blooms for the amount of care they require! An American standard!

Blossom: Blooms are 2" round, white petals with a yellow center, lasting from July to September, especially if deadheaded.

Foliage: Medium green, 3" pointed leaves on very sturdy stems.

Light: Full sun, but does okay with some afternoon shade.

Water: Best in moist, well-drained soil. It may wilt in times of drought but does survive long term.

Use: Great in so many areas where a good-sized flowering plant is needed – as a single clump in the garden, mixed with other summer bloomers such as Black-Eyed Susan, in front of Roses, along a fence as a hedge or just in a bed full of Daisies. Beautiful planted in an area where they are visible in the evening, as the white seems to glow in the dark.

Planting Tips: Loosen the soil well, and add composted material around the roots. Provide plenty of space for them to grow and multiply – they are so worth it!

Fertilizer: Scatter a time-released product, such as Osmocote, or 10-10-10 over the soil in early spring. Also benefits from a new layer of compost.

Plant Support: Staking may become necessary as this plant increases in height and width. Place a large tomato cage around it when it is about a foot tall, or use stakes and string/Velcro tape when it starts to lean over or encroaches into a neighboring plant.

Pruning: Benefits from springtime pruning (Chelsea Chop) to have a tidier, compact plant in the summer. Remove about 6-8" off each stem when they reach about 2'. To keep the plant attractive during bloom time, remove each blossom and its stem as it turns brown down to where it meets the next stem. Trim the stems off completely to the ground in the fall/winter, leaving the leaf clump.

Dividing/Sharing: In either the fall or early spring, with a shovel, dig out a section from the clump or dig up the whole clump, cut into pieces, replant in new areas or share with friends.

Attracts: Butterflies and bees.

Pests/Problems: Aphids may bother this plant. Spray with an insecticidal soap or use a Bayer Advanced Systemic product in early spring. Deer resistant.

Cut Flower: Nice long-stemmed cut flowers by themselves in a vase or add to a mixed bouquet.

Zones: 4-9

Also known as:

Ryan's Daisy, July Daisy.

Gardener's Notes:

_____

_____

_____

_____

As the garden grows, so does the gardener.

– Anonymous

Polygonatum odoratum

Solomon's Seal

Partial shade
Small, white blooms
Variegated leaves
2't, spreads slowly
Deciduous

Solomon's Seal is grown for the bold variegated foliage, which adds a unique texture and brightness to the partly-shaded garden. There are many varieties of this hardy woodland plant, but I enjoy the variegated foliage the most. It grows about 2' tall and spreads slowly. In the spring, it is fun to see the pointed tips popping out of the ground to signal a new season.

Blossom: Small, white, bell-shaped flowers dangle from the leaf nodes for a few weeks in early spring. Fragrant.

Foliage: The medium green leaves have white edges along arching stems that lean downward. Stays fresh and attractive all season with very little care. The foliage turns a nice bright yellow in the fall.

Light: Partial shade – performs well with 2-3 hours of bright light in the morning.

Water: Flourishes with regular watering but is basically very drought tolerant.

Use: Very attractive in a woodland garden or in a shady corner by a foundation. Because it doesn't have heavy feeder roots, it is very useful under trees. Planted with Ferns, Hostas, Epimediums and Lenten Rose, these add a nice contrast in foliage and texture. Especially appealing when the group matures and becomes full – spreads steadily, but not invasive.

Containers: Looks great as a tall element planted with other foliage plants and annuals such as Heucheras, Ferns and White Impatiens.

Planting Tips: Plant in a good, woodsy (well-composted and loose) soil. However, does survive in less than perfect conditions!

Fertilizer: A top dressing of cow manure or any composted material performs well as a fertilizer.

Plant Support: None; allow the natural arching shape to take over.

Pruning: No deadheading is needed for the blooms. After frost, the stems are easy to pull right out of the base.

Dividing/Sharing: Not necessary to divide unless it outgrows its space – dig up the entire clump and separate into smaller sections to replant. To share with a grateful gardener, simply unearth offsets from the outer edges of the plant clump.

Pests/Problems: Deer resistant.

Cut Flower: The arching stems and variegated foliage add a unique texture to any arrangement.

Zones: 4-8

Additional Varieties:
P. biflorum – True Solomon's Seal – very dependable and fast growing.
P. biflorum var. commutatum – Giant Solomon's Seal. Grows about 5' tall.

Gardener's Notes:

_____

_____

_____

_____

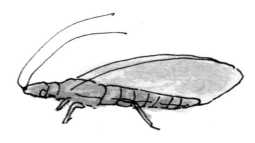

Southern Shield Fern

Part shade to full sun
No bloom
Light green foliage
3-4't and spreading
Deciduous

The Southern Shield Fern, also known as Sun Fern, has the ability to flourish in full sun, making it a favorite among Fern lovers. Spreading, but not invasive – try one and you will have plenty more in years to come!

Foliage: The light green fronds (leaves) have a triangular shape at the top, growing 3-4' tall. In a couple years, a one-gallon plant will triple in size and form a soft, pretty mass. Makes a late appearance in the spring.

Light: Part shade to full sun.

Water: Does fine in dry conditions, but thrives and spreads much faster in moist areas.

Use: Looks great in so many areas: a mass planting along a wall or the back of the garden, two or three next to a gate, a mailbox or tucked into a corner with boulders and large Hostas or Lenten Rose at its feet. Because of the soft look and light green color, it contrasts well with darker, coarser ferns and shrubs.

Planting Tips: The planting area should be loosened and amended with compost. The roots (rhizomes) stay only a few inches from the surface, so make the hole wider than it is deep.

Fertilizer: Adding a layer of organic compost over the plant as it unfurls each spring is all it needs.

Plant Support: Fairly stable, but may need a stake if the wind or a hard rain causes it to topple over.

Pruning: Trim off any broken or browned fronds during the season to keep the plant neat and tidy. After the first frost, cut off all of the plant to the ground. However, some gardeners prefer to leave the browned fronds for the natural look all winter; just trim before new growth appears in the spring.

Dividing/Sharing: A very easy chore! With a shovel, dig up a portion with at least three frond stems growing in it. Replant in a new area, or make a fellow gardener happy!

Pests: Running children and dogs, as with most ferns!

Zones: 5-9

Gardener's Notes:

_____

_____

_____

_____

Oxalis, Lady Fern, Artemisia, Veronica – Sun to Part Shade

Toad Lily

Partial to full shade
White to pink with dark spots
Pale green leaves
2-3't x 2-3'w
Deciduous

Miyazaki Toad Lily is one of the prettiest flowers in shade areas when other summer blooms start to fade. The clump of arching stems is so handsome, even before the beautiful blooms appear. It is one of the last perennials to blossom but is always worth the wait!

Blossom: Similar to an Orchid, the 2" blooms are white or lavender covered with dark purple spots. In early fall, they appear all along the stem at the intersection of the leaves.

Foliage: The 3" oblong, pale green leaves grow on each side of the 2-3' long, arching stems.

Light: Partial to full shade.

Water: Likes moist but well-drained soil. In times of drought, the tips of the leaves may turn brown.

Use: Looks best as a single plant with plenty of room to really show it off. It is especially attractive arching over a pond or other water feature. Plant toward the middle to front of the garden so the blooms can be clearly admired.

Planting Tips: Plant in amended, rich soil with good drainage.

Fertilizer: A time-released product such as Osmocote scattered in the spring when new growth appears is good. Also, add a new layer of compost.

Plant support: None is needed, as it would take away from the attractive relaxed stems.

Pruning: Trimming is not necessary during the season, as the graceful form looks so natural. Prune away everything to the ground after the first frost, if not before, to neaten up the garden.

Dividing/Sharing: This plant can go for years without needing to be divided. But if you want to divide for more plants of your own or to share, do so in early spring by digging up the whole plant and dividing it into a few sections, or just dig a piece away from the side of the mother plant.

Pests/Problems: Voles (buy a cat!).

Cut Flower: So pretty in a vase all by itself to show off the striking little blooms.

Zones: 4-9

Additional Varieties:

White Towers – white blossoms with purple stamens
Miyazaki Gold – similar blossoms to Miyazaki with gold-edged leaves

Gardener's Notes:

_____

_____

_____

_____

> *TIP*
> *Before planting, soak plants in their containers in a bucket of water until saturated – they will adapt to their new home much better.*

Toad Lily – Formosa

Partial shade
Mauve-purple blooms
Glossy, dark green leaves
2-3't x 2'w
Deciduous

The formosana species of Toad Lily is very easy to grow in the woodland or partial-shade garden, spreading by above-ground runners but not invasive. The plant is more upright than the hirta species, with the blooms being similar, small and orchid-like, but held up on the tips of the stem. Begins blooming in mid-summer just when the shady areas need some fresh blooms.

Blossom: A very sweet but exotic 1" mauve-purple bloom with a white throat and dark spots that lasts for many weeks into the fall. Resembles a small orchid bloom.

Foliage: Glossy leaves are dark green, mottled with purple-green spots.

Light: Partial shade, looking its best with a few hours of morning sun.

Water: Regular watering as drought and excessive heat can cause the leaf tips to turn brown. Wet feet in the winter can cause root rot.

Use: Plant toward the front of the garden to enjoy the blooms up close. Planting among other partial shade lovers, such as Heucheras, Hostas and Ferns, will help to showcase the loose foliage as well as the small blossoms.

Planting Tips: Prepare the area with soil conditioner, compost, etc. to achieve a loose, woodsy soil.

Fertilizer: A new 1/2" layer of compost (manure or soil conditioner) is always beneficial spread over the plant in early spring. A time-released fertilizer also works well.

Plant Support: May need a single-ring stake to hold it up if it is in too much shade and starts to lean over.

Pruning: Trim off to the ground in late fall.

Dividing/Sharing: Easy to divide by digging a clump away from the mother plant.

Pests/Problems: Voles – they eat the roots! Call in the cats! Slugs may appear in moist conditions; use a slug bait for best results.

Cut Flower: So pretty in a small vase by itself or with the lacy foliage of Luxuriant Bleeding Heart.

Zones: 4-9

Additional Varieties:

Alba – white blooms

Gardener's Notes:

_____

_____

_____

_____

Veronica

Full sun to part shade
Blue-purple blossom
Green foliage
1-3't x 1-3'w
Deciduous

Veronica has many showy species, from upright plants to low-growing. I am discussing the easy-to-grow group known as Speedwells, as they are the most readily available in nurseries. The names of the species keep changing, so experiment with what you can find!

Blossom: Showy bottle-brush-like spikes of flowers from early summer to late fall. Available in shades of pink and white, with the blue-purple varieties the most common.

Foliage: Medium to dark green leaves that are lance-shaped, often crinkled and form a shrubby plant.

Light: Full sun to part shade.

Water: Consistent watering is best. Because of their shallow roots, supplemental water is needed during drought conditions. That said, wet feet in the winter may cause root rot.

Use: A pretty texture and useful height for the summer garden. Plant in groups of at least three to five to make a statement. Especially attractive in front of the yellow blooms of Black-Eyed Susan, white Shasta Daisies, Yarrows or Butterfly Weed. Useful as an edging along a walkway or the front of a bed. The spikes add a significant element to any container.

Planting Tips: Not too fussy about the soil conditions. Dig a good-sized hole, placing the top of the crown slightly below the soil level because of its shallow roots. A rich soil may cause too much growth and the plant will flop over!

Plant Support: The tomato cage type of support is needed with the taller varieties as they tend to lean or collapse if in too much shade.

Pruning: After the first flush of blooms, force yourself to trim off the fading spikes of flowers. This will increase the production of more blooms into late summer and early fall.

Fertilizer: Average planting soil and a compost/mulch covering is usually sufficient.

Dividing/Sharing: Divide in the spring or fall every few years, removing any dead portions.

Pests/Problems: Powdery mildew seems to be the biggest problem in humid regions. Trim off infected areas after blooming and it should perk back up. Keep the soil from drying out.

Cut Flower: The upright spiky blooms are a perfect addition to any arrangement.

Zones: 3-8

A Few of the Available Varieties:

Giles van Hees – rose-pink, 6-8"
Goodness Grows – dark violet-blue, 1-1.5'
Icicle – white, 2+'
Pink Panther – lilac, 2'
Sunny Border Blue – dark violet-blue, 1-1.5' (mildew resistant)

Gardener's Notes:

_____

_____

_____

_____

_____

_____

Yarrow

Full sun
Blooms June-August
Aromatic foliage
2't and spreading
Deciduous

Common Yarrow is a summer-blooming perennial you can always count on to add nice airy foliage and a wide range of blossom colors to your garden. Vigorous, invasive for some gardeners, depending on your outlook!

Blossoms: The blooms are showy, flattened heads made up of tiny daisy flowers, approximately 2-3" round. Color selections range from rosy hues to reds to yellow. The blooms last from early to late summer, fading with age.

Foliage: Soft, feathery, dark green leaves add a delicate texture to the sunny garden. Aromatic.

Light: Full sun.

Water: Moist soil as long as it is well drained. Also thrives in sandy or dry conditions.

Use: Looks great in the middle of the perennial garden in a grouping of at least three plants. Plant annuals or shorter perennials in front of Yarrow to hide leggy stems that may appear by the end of the season.

Planting Tips: The soil should be well drained and not too rich – this encourages lush plants without much sturdiness. Give plants plenty of space to spread out – good air circulation is a necessity.

Fertilizer: Each spring, use an organic fertilizer or 10-10-10 lightly sprinkled around the new growth.

Plant Support: If plants get leggy, use stakes to hold them erect or to keep them from leaning into neighboring plants.

Pruning: Trim off the faded flower heads and stems down to the foliage to tidy up the plant as well as encourage new growth and blossoms later in the season.

Dividing/Sharing: As new growth appears in the spring, or after the stems have been cut down in the fall, dig up clumps and runners. Should be divided every few years to clean out the weak plants.

Attracts: Butterflies.

Pests: None.

Cut Flower: Cut stems when half of the flowers have opened, remove lower leaves and slit the stems. Very nice with other summer blossoms. To dry the blossoms, hang upside down in a warm, dry spot.

Zones: 3-9

A Few Favorites:
Fire King – red
Paparika – orange-red
Rose Beauty – rosy hues
Galaxy Series

Gardener's Notes:

_____

_____

_____

_____

_____

_____

_____

Yarrow – Fernleaf

Full sun
Yellow-gold blooms
Grey-green foliage
2-3't x 2-3'w
Deciduous

Fernleaf Yarrow is a very hardy, long-lasting plant that can thrive in poor soils and extended periods of heat. This is definitely a plant you can always count on – the upright clump of foliage, yellow blooms and herbal aroma adds so much to any landscape.

Blossom: All shades of yellow, 2-3" large flat clusters on very stiff stems in spring and summer.

Foliage: The Fernleaf varieties have soft, deeply-cut foliage that has a grey-green cast, adding a good contrast even when not in bloom. The pleasant aroma is a bonus.

Light: Full sun. Becomes leggy and will collapse in too much shade.

Water: Drought resistant once established. Does not perform well in wet soil.

Use: Best planted as a solo (specimen) to really show off the soft foliage and blossoms of this clump-forming perennial. Plant in the middle-back area of a bed, near a mailbox or against large boulders.

Planting Tips: The biggest requirement is to plant in loose soil, on the dry side. Do not plant in low or moist areas; make sure it has excellent drainage.

Fertilizer: Amending the soil with compost is all the fertilizer this plant needs. Overdoing the fertilizer causes the plant to grow too tall and collapse.

Plant Support: A large round tomato cage or similar support is perfect, especially if planted in part shade. Place the cage around the plant when it is about 1' tall.

Pruning: Trimming off the spent flower heads down to the next side (lateral) bud may encourage new blooms. These browned blossoms can be left on or trimmed off if not attractive to you. Remove all stems down to ground (basal) foliage before frost, or earlier, to tidy up the garden.

Dividing/Sharing: Dig up the clump and divide every three to four years in early spring to keep the plant healthy. Replant in your yard or share!

Attracts: Bees, butterflies and birds.

Pests/Problems: Deer resistant. Planting in heavy clay soils will result in root rot.

Cut Flower: To use in an arrangement, cut off when the flower heads are half opened. Remove the lower leaves and split the stems with a knife. Also very nice for dried arrangements later in the season when fully opened – hang upside down to dry out.

Zones: 3-8

Favorite Varieties:
    Anthea – sulfur yellow, 2' tall
    Coronation Gold – mustard yellow, 2-3' tall
    Moonshine – bright yellow, 12-18" tall

Gardener's Notes:

_____

_____

_____

_____

_____

_____

The Wedding of the Flowers

At the wedding of the flowers
The guests arrived in PHLOX.
The place was in the garden,
The time was FOUR-O'CLOCK.

The OLD-MAID and the BACHELOR'S BUTTON
Were going to be wed,
And I never was so startled
As when the flowers left their bed.

The OLD-MAID wore her BRIDAL WREATH
On a wig of MAIDENHAIR,
With LADY'S SLIPPERS on her feet,
My! How the flowers did stare.

But all dressed up in JOSEPH'S COAT
With a TURK'S-CAP on his head,
The BACHELOR'S BUTTON was a sight
For one about to wed.

VIOLET with her BABY'S BREATH
And eyes of CORNFLOWER blue,
Was chosen maid of honor
Instead of BLACK-EYED Sue.

While WEDDING BELLS rang softly
ROSE sang FORGET-ME-NOT
Then the WILLOW started weeping
Right there on the spot.

While JACK-IN-THE-PULPIT read the vows
SWEET WILLIAM held the ring,
But the best man, JOHNNY-JUMP-UP,
Shook like everything.

The bridesmaids were the DAISIES
All dressed in QUEEN ANNE'S LACE.
But the SUNFLOWERS shone so brightly
They had to shade their face.

Now if anyone should wonder
How the flowers left the sod,
It was PRINCE'S-FEATHER'S magic—
He waved his GOLDENROD.

— Jacqueline Letchworth

Beneficial Insects

Lacewing
Adult

Larva

Assassin Bug

Common Name: Assassin Bug

Type of Insect: True Bug – reduviidae

Size: 1/2" to 1"

Color: Dark brown, black or reddish

Habitat: Overwinter in garden depris; lays eggs in soil, under stones or on leaves

Purpose: Adults and nymphs feed on the larvae and adult insects of aphids, beetles, caterpillars, flies and leafhoppers. A predator you really want in your garden.

Host Plants: Perennial weeds, flower and vegetable blossoms

Bumblebee

Common Name: Bumblebee

Type of Insect: Bee – Bombus spp.

Size: 1/2" to 1"

Color: Brownish-orange to black with yellow bands

Habitat: Existing mouse burrows or natural cavities in ground or rock walls

Purpose: Important pollinators

Host Plants: Perennial weeds, flower and vegetable blossoms

Dragonfly

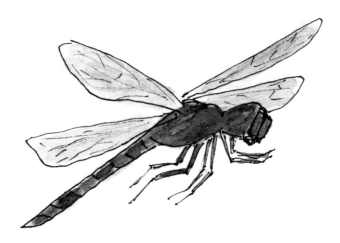

Common Name: Dragonfly*

Type of Insect: Odonata – Gomphidae

Size: 2" to 6"

Color: Green, yellow, black, blue – irredescent in some species

Habitat: Ponds, lakes, rivers, streams, swamps – some species hunt their prey some distance from water

Purpose: Predator of mosquitoes, flies, bees, ants

Host Plants: Water and water vegitation required for mating and larvae

* The order Odonata is made up of Dragonflies, Damselflies, Darners, Biddies and Skimmers. These families contain hundreds of species. They all look very much alike, however, they differ in size and color, how they catch their prey, how and when they mate, and how they hold their wings when stationary.

Flower Hover Fly

Common Name: Flower Hover Fly

Type of Insect: Fly – Syrphidae

Size: 3/8" to 5/8"

Color: Shiny with black abdomens, yellow or white bands, reddish eyes

Habitat: Overwinter in the soil; females lay eggs in aphid colonies

Purpose: One larvae can eat 400 aphids

Host Plants: Ajuga, lavendar, yarrow, dill, fennel, Queen Anne's lace, wild chamomile

Ground Beetle

Common Name: Ground Beetle

Type of Insect: Beetle – Carabidae

Size: 3/4" to 1"

Color: Iridescent bluish or purplish black larvae, black or brown

Habitat: Active at night; hides under rocks or in soil crevices during the day

Purpose: Adults and larvae are beneficial predators of cutworms, fly eggs, maggots, snails, slugs, other soft-bodied larvae and pupae found in the soil.

Host Plants: Ground covers and mulches; permanent plantings

Honey Bee

Common Name: Honey Bee

Type of Insect: Bee – apis mellifera

Size: 1/2" to 3/4"

Color: Golden yellow with darker stripes

Habitat: Human-engineered hive boxes or trees

Purpose: Important pollinators

Host Plants: Flowering fruit and vegetable blossoms

Lacewing

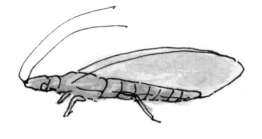

Lacewing Adult

Larvae

Common Name: Lacewing

Type of Insect: Lacewing – chrysopa spp

Size: 1/2" to 3/4"

Color: Adults are light green or beige; larvae tan or grey; alligator shaped

Habitat: Overwinter in garden debris; adults lay eggs among host insects

Purpose: Larvae eat aphids, mites, scales, small caterpillars, thrips, other soft-bodied insects and insect eggs.

Host Plants: Plant pollen and nectar flowers; coriander, dill, daisies, fennel, Queen Anne's lace, yarrow

Lady Beetle

Common Name: Lady Beetle Convergent

Type of Insect: Lady Beetle – hippodamia convergens

Size: 3/8"

Color: Orange or red with black spots. Larvae are alligator shaped. Other species are gray, pale yellow, orange or red with or without spots.

Habitat: Overwinter in garden debris or protected sites

Purpose: Important predators of aphids, insect eggs, mealybugs, scales, small caterpillars and whitefly nymphs

Host Plants: Plant pollen and nectar flowers; queen anne's lace, dandelion, yarrow. Spray sugar water on plants that aphids usually attack – 5 oz. sugar to 1 qt. water.

Mason Bees

Common Name: Orchard Mason Bee; Blue Orchard Bee

Type of Insect: Bee – Osmia lignaria

Size: 1/2"

Color: Bluish black

Habitat: Tree holes, hollow plant stems, cracks under building siding, human-engineered nesting blocks

Purpose: Important pollinators

Host Plants: Blossoms of fruit and nut orchards, dandelion, mustard, pussy willow and other early spring flowers

Multi-Color Asian Lady Beetle

Common Name: Multi-Colored Asian Lady Beetle

Type of Insect: Lady Beetle – Harmonia axyridis

Size: 1/4"

Color: Yellow-orange to reddish-orange; with or without spots; larvae are alligator shaped

Habitat: South side of buildings, rock outcrops

Purpose: Adults and larvae feed on aphids and other soft-bodied insects

Host Plants: Plant pollen and nectar flowers

Note: Sold commercially. There are species of lady beetles that are specialty predators.

Parsley Worm Caterpillar

Parsley Worm
Caterpillar

Larve of
Black
Swallowtail

Common Name: Parsley Worm (Black Swallowtail Butterfly)

Type of Insect: Larvae – of butterfly

Size: Caterpillar is up to 1-1/2"
Swallowtail Butterfly has 3" wingspan

Color: Caterpillar is green with black bands or white or orange spots
Swallowtail Butterflly is black or black with yellow spots

Habitat: White

Purpose: Important pollinators

Host Plants: Flowering fruits and vegetables blossoms

Praying Mantis

Common Name: Praying Mantis

Type of Insect: Mantid – mantidae

Size: 2-3"

Color: Adults are green or brown

Habitat: Eggs overwinter in cases attached to stems; one generation per year

Purpose: Mantids have big appetites and will feed on beneficials like bees and butterflies as well as pests and destructive insects

Host Plants: Throughout the garden

Note: Sold commercially – do not buy eggs for release due to the indiscriminate bug snacking

Rove Beetle

Common Name: Rove Beetle

Type of Insect: Beetle – Staphylinidae

Size: Up to 1"

Color: Dark brown or black; larvae are dark, elongated, and very fast

Habitat: Garden; most active at night

Purpose: Adults and larvae are beneficial, feeding on fly eggs, maggots, nematores, slugs, snails, springtails and other soil-dwelling organisms.

Host Plants: Ground covers and mulches, permanent plantings

Larvae

Soldier Beetle

Common Name: Soldier Beetle/Pennsylvania Leatherwing

Type of Insect: Beetle – Chauliognathus pennsylvanicus

Size: 1/2"

Color: Dull yellowish-orange with black head and legs

Habitat: Garden soil

Purpose: Adults and larvae are beneficial, feeding on grasshopper eggs, rootworks, cucumber beetles, earworms and caterpillars.

Host Plants: Pollen and nectar plants; Leatherwings like goldenrod

Crocosmia, Yarrow, Lamb's Ear – Sun to Part Shade

Accent pieces for the Garden

Perennials are wonderful, but sometimes a few accent pieces or focal points can add a great deal of interest and stability to the garden. Try to make the piece coordinate with the surroundings: rustic with a cottage garden, cement with a formal garden, modern with an eclectic look.

Here is a list of items that can be utilized effectively (just don't overdo it – very easy to get carried away and create a "Wally World" look!!).

Arbor – wooden or metal

Bench – wooden, metal or cement

Bird bath – a deep one is best for the bathing birds; place a rock in the center for smaller birds to sit on

Bird house – a large white one always looks good

Bird feeder – just don't put one in the middle of a flower bed; the seeds sprout grass, and squirrels trample the plants hunting for seeds

Boulders – sink in the ground a bit for a natural look

Containers – make sure the color and composition complement the area

Decorative stakes

Fence – wooden, wrought iron

Gate

Statuary – cement, metal

Stepping stones – plant ground covers in between

Sun dial

Trellis

Wheelbarrow – can be a container!

Blue Fescue, Cheddar Pinks, Angelina Sedum – Sun

Seasonal Calendar of Chores

For perennials to look their best, there are chores that need to be done – some seasonally, others on a weekly basis. Once the spring tasks are done, spending ten minutes a day will help you stay ahead of weeding, deadheading, etc. – you'll be amazed how much you can get done in this amount of time!

Basic chores should include:

Soil preparation
Planting – digging an adequate hole
Fertilize/compost
Dividing
Transplanting
Weeding
Watering
Deadheading
Trimming
Pest control
Clean-up of debris

Then, ENJOY AND ADMIRE YOUR WORK!!

Note: This calendar should be adjusted according to your region's climate and environmental issues. Keep a record of your own seasonal and weekly chores as a guide for future seasons.

Late Winter

Take advantage of nice days by removing debris of twigs, matted fallen leaves that are covering early spring arrivals, and winter weeds.

Make notes on the look of the garden in the winter – does it need more evergreen shrubs, a rock wall, boulders, a birdbath, a birdhouse, etc.? Always be planning for next year!

Lenten Rose: trim off older, dark leaves at the base to show off new growth and the blooms.

Muhly Grass: trim back to 3-4" tall before new growth begins.

Roses: trim back the oldest canes, usually brown in color, to the ground. Trim others to about half the desired summer height.

Bird houses: clean out so they will be ready to welcome your new spring guests!

Early Spring

The perfect time to have your soil tested through your local Extension Office.

Clean up all debris (twigs, leaves, acorns, etc. – places insects can hide!) in garden areas.

Make sure the soil is dry enough to work with – it should crumble in your hand when squeezed. Do not trample newly-planted areas as this will compact the soil.

Check for any low-lying areas that tend to hold water and adjust the soil level.

Purchase bags of compost/soil conditioner or use your own to prepare new beds/planting holes and add to existing areas.

Time to divide and transplant – easiest to do when the new foliage starts popping out of the ground.

Trim and clean up any evergreen plants that have winter damage.

Spring

Busiest time of year for the gardener as well as the plants!

Plant new additions to the garden and water well. Use a root stimulant product, such Quick-Start, to help with the transition. Also good for transplants.

Spread new compost and or mulch.

Time for the "Chelsea Chop" for many perennials – Daisy, Phlox, Asters, etc. Once the plant reaches about half its mature height, trim off at least one-quarter. This takes courage – they will bloom just fine and be much sturdier plants!

Fill in gaps in the garden with annuals for continuous color, once the chance of frost has passed.

Plant containers – use a variety of tall, medium and short perennials along with annuals. Include interesting textures and colors of foliage. Use a liquid root stimulant and then fertilize with a water-soluble product every two weeks for great results.

Watch out for summer weeds and pests – they are now making their appearance!

Summer

Additional water is usually needed – try to do this in the morning to prevent evaporation.

Deadhead (remove spent blossoms/foliage/stems) to encourage more growth and to keep a tidy-looking garden.

Feed your plants, especially if the rainfall has been abundant and washed away nutrients. Use a liquid mix product, such as Miracle Gro, so as not to burn or over-do in the heat.

Pest control – watch for any damage by insects and treat accordingly. Usually insecticidal soap will treat the problem without harming the "good bugs."

Weed – best done by hand or with a small garden fork, by pulling out the foliage along with the root. Weeds compete for nutrients, sunlight and water. And yes, you will learn the difference between weeds and perennials, it just takes experience.

Take notes and pictures on performance, spacing, colors, light issues, etc., to make plans for any transplanting that needs to be done in the fall.

Fall

Continue to water, as warm fall days can dry out the soil.

Keep pulling the weeds – less seed heads means fewer weeds next year.

Best time to divide and transplant as well as plant new perennials. Remember to add amendments to the planting area and dig a good-sized hole.

Try to keep the labels with the plants, or make a diagram – this will help to identify the plant and the location.

Trim back any perennials that have finished blooming and discard – leaving debris on the ground encourages hiding places for the "bad bugs" and creatures!

Spread a layer of compost (shredded leaves, etc.) around the plants' base for winter nutrition and protection.

Time to put the garden to bed – finish cleaning up, trimming, taking notes for future projects.

ENJOY THE LATE FALL GARDEN with its clean appearance. The evergreens, trees, rock walls, benches, trellises are now the stars of your landscape – until spring, that is!

Phlox, Iris – Sun

My garden of flowers is also my garden of thoughts and dreams.

– Abram L. Urban

USDA MAP

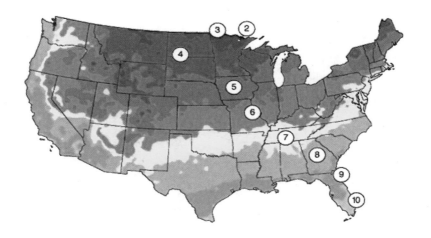

Zones: The United States is divided into Plant Hardiness Zones by the USDA. Locate your region on this map to determine your own zone. This will aid you in choosing plants suited to survive the expected low winter temperatures in your area. All degrees are Farenheit.

Zone 2 -50° to -40°
Zone 3 -40° to -30°
Zone 4 -30° to -20°
Zone 5 -20° to -10°
Zone 6 -10° to 0°
Zone 7 0° to 10°
Zone 8 10° to 20°
Zone 9 20° to 30°
Zone 10 30° to 40°

Pink Muhly Grass, Fairy Rose – Sun

What is a garden

Large or small

'Tis just a garden,

after all.

– Reginald Arkell

Common Gardening Terms

Amend the soil: to add material, such as compost, pine straw, mulched leaves, etc., to enrich the soil before planting.

Annuals: plants that grow and flower in a single season.

Bed: an area of soil prepared for planting.

Berm: an area that is built up with soil to raise the height of the plants.

Border: a garden bed that lies adjacent to an element that forms a boundary for the bed, such as a walkway, patio, hedge, fence, rock out-cropping, etc.

Cane: a main stem that grows from the base of the plant. Rose stems are usually called canes.

Compost: a collection of leaves, grass clippings, manure and vegetable matter that is left to decay for about a year. It makes an excellent soil amendment, fertilizer as well as mulch.

Crown: the part of the plant, usually at ground level, between the root and the stem.

Cutting garden: a garden bed set aside for producing flowers specifically for cutting.

Deadheading: same as pinching back. Removing the spent blooms so the plant uses its energy to produce new, vigorous blooms and growth. Also keeps them looking neat.

Deciduous: woody plants that drop their leaves annually (Roses, Phlox, Maple Trees, etc.).

Dormant: temporarily inactive growing season, usually late fall-winter, and the preferred time for planting.

Drainage: cultivation of soil to allow liquid to filter slowly through the soil instead of allowing the soil to hold water.

Espalier: training of trees or vines to grow in formal, two-dimensional forms against a wall or fence.

Evergreen: plants with foliage that persists and remains green throughout the year.

Fertilize: feeding the plants with chemical or organic nutrients.

Flats: shallow plastic box used to start seeds or hold a multitude of small plants.

Full shade: a site that does not receive any direct sunlight. A suitable garden area with full shade should receive good indirect light all day long. Sites that do not, such as under evergreens, will not support plants.

Full sun: a site that receives ten hours of direct, uninterrupted sunlight per day. Many plants that require full sun will grow well with 7-8 hours of direct sunlight.

Fungicide: a liquid or powder used to control fungi. An effective organic fungicide is a spray made from one teaspoon baking soda and a drop of dishwashing liquid per quart of water.

Ground cover: a low-growing plant that is grown for the purpose of covering an area with a mass of foliage.

Hardiness Zones: refers to a plant's ability to withstand cold, heat, wind, humidity or altitudes and to survive.

Heaving: bulging out of the ground after a hard freeze; danger of exposing roots.

Herbaceous: grass-like quality of foliage.

Humus: brown or black organic substance consisting of partially- or wholly-decayed matter that provides nutrients for plants and increases the ability of soil to retain water.

Island: freestanding area, usually surrounded by lawn.

Limbing up: removing the lower limbs or branches of a shrub or tree to improve its overall appearance. Allows light into the area below, which makes room for more planting!

Manure: animal feces used for fertilizer because of the humus it contains. Manure must be rotted or composted before using, or it will burn plants.

Mildew: a group of fungal diseases characterized by powdery white or grayish patches on plant leaves.

Mixed border: an area planted with perennials, annuals as well as trees and shrubs.

Mulch: protective covering (pine needles, shredded bark, compost) placed around plants to prevent evaporation of moisture, freezing of roots, and multiplying of weeds.

Ornamentals: plants that are grown for use other than eating.

Partial shade: a site that is in shade for part of the day and full sun for the remaining daylight hours. In general, more shade than sun.

Partial sun: a site that is in sun for part of the day and shade for the remaining daylight hours. In general, more sun than shade.

Peat moss: a very water-retentive, organic soil amendment composed of partially decomposed remains of any of several mosses.

Perennials: plants that have a life span of more than two years. (Iris, Daisies, Daylilies, etc.)

pH: measurement of the soil's alkaline or acid level – sweet or sour characteristics.

Pinching back: the act of nipping off stems/foliage in order to encourage fuller plants and more blooms (deadheading).

Prune: to remove growth from a plant in order to direct its size and shape, remove diseased or damaged wood, maintain health and vigor and control flowering.

Semi-evergreen: retaining some green leaves through the winter.

Shade: the degree of light without direct sunlight. Light is necessary for even the most shade-loving plants.

Specimen: a single plant grown in a conspicuous location in the garden, making a significant impact.

Standard: a plant trained to resemble a small tree, with a single, upright trunk topped by a rounded crown of foliage.

Tap root: a root system that has a single main root with smaller roots branching off it.

Top dress: to apply fertilizer or compost on top of the soil.

Top soil: the fertile soil, humus mixed with mineral soil, in which plants grow.

Variegated: a leaf marked with stripes, edges, spots or blotches of cream, white or another color.

Wildflower: a flowering plant that grows in an uncultivated area.

Winter over: to prepare a plant by wrapping, shielding or mulching so that it will be protected through the winter freeze.

Woodland: a shady area with shrubs and trees forming a canopy.

Suggested Light Requirements

(to aid in site selection of your perennials)

Note: It takes some trial and error, but many perennials will adjust their needs to where they are planted. For example, I have Black-Eyed Susan planted in both full sun and part shade – the part-shade plant blooms just fine, but a week or so later than its friend in full sun. The same with low-growing sedums – they just don't grow as large when planted in the shade. As they say, plants don't read what they are "supposed" to do!

Full sun:

Ajuga

Artemisia

Aster

Blackberry Lily

Black-Eyed Susan

Blue Fescue Grass

Brown-Eyed Susan

Butterfly Weed

Cheddar Pinks

Coreopsis

Crocosmia

Fairy Rose

Ghenghis Kahn Aster

Goldenrod

Iris

Knock Out Rose

Oxalis

Phlox

Pink Muhly Grass

Purple Coneflower

Sedum

Shasta Daisy

Southern Shield Fern

Veronica

Yarrow

Part shade-part sun – these perennials can usually tolerate a few hours of morning sun, just don't let them be exposed to the western afternoon sun:

Ajuga

Astilbe

Autumn Fern

Bleeding Heart

Ghost Fern

Green and Gold

Heuchera

Hosta

Japanese Painted Fern

Lady Fern

Lenten rose

Oxalis

Sedum – Low Growing

Solomon's Seal

Toad Lily

Variegated Holly Fern

Full shade:

Autumn Fern

Bleeding Heart

Ghost Fern

Holly Fern

Hosta

Japanese Painted Fern

Lady Fern

Lenten Rose

Solomon's Seal

Toad Lily

Variegated Holly Fern

TIP
To attract bluebirds, place mealy worms (available at your local birding store) in a saucer in the yard, same time every day – they will be waiting for you!

Southern Shield Fern, Yarrow, Ajuga – Sun

Common Names Index

Botanical Names Index

Botanical Pronunciation Guide

Note: this information differs from source to source. This list is from *Taylor's Guides.*

Achillea filipendulina   *uh-KILL-ee-uh fil-ih-pen-due-LEE-nuh*   Fernleaf Yarrow

Achillea millefolium   *ah-KILL-ee-ah mil-leh-FOE-lee-um*   Common Yarrow

Ajuga reptans   *ah-JEW-guh REP-tanz*   Bugleweed

Arachniodes simplicior   *a-rak-nee-OH-dees sim-PLIK-ee-or*   Variegated Holly Fern

Artemisia   *are-teh-MEE-see-uh*   Wormwood

Asclepias tuberosa   *as-KLEE-pee-us too-ber-OH-suh*   Butterfly Weed

Asteromoea mongolica   *ass-ter-OH-mee-uh mon-GOL-ik-uh*   Ghenghis Kahn Aster

Aster   *ASS-ter*

Astilbe arendsii   *uh-STILL-bee uh-REND-zee-eye*   False Spirea

Astilbe chinensis   *uh-STILL-bee chih-NEN-sis*   Chinese Astilbe

Athyrium   *ah-THY-ree-um*   Ghost Fern

Athyrium filix-femina   *ah-THY-ree-um FEE-lix-FEM-in-uh*   Lady Fern

Athyrium nipponicum   *ah-THY-ree-um nih-PON-ih-kum*   Japanese Painted Fern

Belamcanda   *beh-lam-KAN-duh*   Blackberry Lily

Chrysogonum virginianum   *kry-SOG-oh-num ver-jin-ee-AH-num*   Green and Gold

Coreopsis auriculata   *kore-ee-OP-sis aw-rick-yew-LAH-tuh*   Tickseed Coreopsis

Coreopsis verticillata   *kore-ee-OP-sis ver-tih-sil-LAH-tuh*   Threadleaf Coreopsis

Crocosmia   *kroh-KOS-mee-uh*   Montbretia

Cyrtomium falcatum   *sear-TOE-mee-um fal-KAY-tum*   Holly Fern

Dianthus gratianopolitanus   *dye-AN-thuss grah-tee-ah-no-pol-ih-TAY-nus*   Cheddar Pinks

Dicentra eximia   *dye-SEN-truh ex-EE-meh-uh*   Fernleaf Bleeding Heart

Dicentra spectabilis   *dye-SEN-truh spek-TAB-ih-liss*   Common Bleeding Heart

Dryopteris erythrosora   *dry-OP-ter-iss er-rith-roh-SOR-uh*   Autumn Fern

Echinacea purpurea   *eck-in-AY-see-uh pur-PUR-ee-ah*   Purple Coneflower

Festuca glauca   *fess-TOO-kuh GLAW-kuh*   Blue Fescue Grass

Helleborous orientalis   *hel-eh-BORE-us or-ee-en-TAL-iss*   Lenten Rose

Heuchera villosa   *HEW-ker-uh vil-OH-suh*   Coral Bells, Alum Root

Hosta   *HOSS-tuh*   Plantain Lily

Iridaceae   *eye-rid-AY-see-ee*   Tall Beared Iris

Leucanthemum x superbum   *loo-KAN-thuh-mum sue-PER-bum*   Shasta Daisy

Muhlenbergia capillaris   *mew-len-BERG-gee-uh kap-ill-AR-iss*   Pink Muhly Grass

Oxalis   *ox-AL-iss*   Oxalis

Phlox paniculata   *pan-ick-you-LAH-tuh*   Phlox

Polygonatum odoratum   *pah-lig-oh-NAY-tum oh-door-AH-tum*   Fragrant Solomon's Seal

Rosa Polyantha   *ROE-suh pol-ee-ANTH-uh*   The Fairy Rose

Rudbeckia fulgida   *rude-BEK-ee-uh FUL-jih-duh*   Black-Eyed Susan

Rudbeckia Triloba   *rude-BEK-ee-uh try-LO-buh*   Brown-Eyed Susan

Sedum   *SEE-dum*   Stonecrop (Low-growing, Upright)

Solidago   *sol-ih-DAY-go*   Goldenrod

Stachys byzantina   *STAY-kuss bih-zan-TEE-nuh*   Lamb's Ears

Thelypteris kunthii   *the-LIP-ter-is KUN-thee-eye*   Southern Shield Fern

Tricyrtis formosana   *try-SIR-tiss for-moh-SAH-nuh*   Toad Lily formosansa

Tricyrtis hirta   *try-SIR-tiss HUR-tuh*   Toad Lily hirta

Veronica   *ver-AH-nih-kuh*   Veronica Speedwell

Bibliography/Additional Reading

References are necessary in compiling any good garden book. I recommend the following books for additional information on perennials.

Armitage, Allan. Armitage's Garden Perennials: A Color Encyclopedia. Portland, OR: Timber Press, 2000.

Bender, Steve (ed.). The Southern Living Garden Book. Birmingham, AL: Oxmoor House, 2004.

Botanica. Annuals & Perennials. San Diego, CA: Laurel Glen Publishing, 1999.

Glasener, Erica, and Walter Reeves. Georgia Gardener's Guide. Franklin, TN: Cool Springs Press, 1996.

Halpin, Anne, and Betty Mackey. Cutting Gardens. New York, NY: Simon & Schuster, 1993.

Macunovich, Janet. Caring for Perennials. Pownal, VT: Storey Books, 1997.

Phillips, Ellen, and C. Colston Burrell. Rodale's Illustrated Encyclopedia of Perennials. Emmaus, PA: St. Martin's Press, 1993.

Smith, Miranda, and Ana Carr. Rodale's Garden Insect & Weed Identification Guide. Emmaus, PA: Rodale Press, 1988.

Tenenbaum, Frances (ed.). Taylor's Guides, Encyclopedia of Garden Plants. New York, NY: Houghton Mifflin, 2003.

Valleau, John M. Perennial Gardening Guide. Abbotsford, British Columbia: Valleybrook International Ventures, 2003.

Author and Illustrator Biographies

About the Author

Althea Griffin is a lifelong gardener whose knowledge of plants and eye for design led to the formation of a co-owned landscape design business, Garden Gals, in Atlanta, Georgia. She has gardened her way from Vermont to Ohio to Georgia, learning and enjoying it every step of the way. Her gardens have been featured on garden tours in the Atlanta area. Althea is married and has two children and four grandchildren, to whom she hopes to pass along her love of gardening.

About the Illustrator

Kate Ruland, an architectural draftsman by trade, has also studied watercolor, pastel drawing and sculpture at The Southern Vermont Art Center. She is a lifelong organic gardener and is devoted to composting. Kate and her sisters, Lisa and Althea, inherited their green thumbs and love of plants from their maternal grandmother, Katherine Dahl Marino. The illustrations in this book are dedicated to her.

Ordering Information

To order additional copies of

Perennials...What you need to know!

and for information on purchasing

Ink and Watercolor Illustrations

by Kate Ruland, please visit

http://www.PerennialsWhatYouNeedToKnow.com.